RETRIEVAL PRACTICE 2

Implementing, embedding & reflecting

KATE JONES

First Published 2021

by John Catt Educational Ltd,
15 Riduna Park, Melton, Woodbridge, Suffolk IP12 1QT
01394 389850
enquiries@johncatt.com
www.johncatt.com

Tel: +44 (0) 1394 389850
Fax: +44 (0) 1394 386893
Email: enquiries@johncatt.com
Website: www.johncatt.com

ISBN: 978 1 91362 241 1

Set and designed by John Catt Educational Limited

A special dedication to Professors Robert Bjork and Elizabeth Bjork for your support and helping me to become a better teacher.

2020 was a challenging year for us all and 2021 continues to test us. I would also like to dedicate this book to the staff and students at The British School Al Khubairat (BSAK) in Abu Dhabi, United Arab Emirates. I am incredibly grateful to work at such a wonderful school.

Thank you to all the people that have contributed to this book. Thanks to friends, family and colleagues for your continued support.

PRAISE FOR RETRIEVAL PRACTICE 2

Sequels can often leave you disappointed and reflecting that it isn't as good as the original. However, in the case of Kate Jones' follow up to *Retrieval Practice: Research & Resources for every classroom*, this is a phenomenal follow on. As Kate outlines in the beginning of the book, the concept of retrieval practice has now become a feature of many classrooms and the next step is now about reflecting on its implementation and how to embed it further. Kate takes you on a journey, reflecting on current implementation of retrieval practice, the common pitfalls, and the ever-growing research and reflections from researchers. Whilst the final chapter brings together all of this with a range of examples from different subjects making this a fantastic toolkit for all teachers. Retrieval practice is quite rightly recognised as a powerful learning strategy and this book provides great insight into embedding this essential strategy to boost learning for your pupils. I highly recommend it.

Michael Chiles, Geography Trust Lead at King's Leadership Academy and author of *The CRAFT of Assessment* **and** *The Feedback Pendulum* **(@m_chiles)**

If you try out one new learning strategy in your classroom this year, make it retrieval practice. And what better way to get it right than by reading Kate Jones' books? Her first book *Retrieval Practice: Research & Resources for every classroom* is packed full of ideas, resources and strategies while this second book strengthens and deepens the links between academia and the classroom. Kate looks at the research behind those strategies in more detail and brings it to life in a way that makes sense to all. In her latest book, Kate has gathered together insights and suggestions from eminent researchers in the field of memory and specifically retrieval practice, who share how they see retrieval practice making a difference to students. In her easy-to-read style, Kate helps you take not just your first step towards becoming a research-informed teacher, but also your second, third and fourth. We love the case studies from classroom practitioners and the focus on our current Covid-19 restrictions. All in all, this second book is a must read for any educator focused on making a difference to learning.

**Jane Miller and Finola Wilson,
Directors of Impact Wales & former teachers (@ImpactWales)**

Retrieval Practice 2 is essential reading for all educators. In a clear and accessible way, Kate brings to life the latest research on retrieval practice and how to harness this powerful learning strategy in the classroom with maximal effectiveness. If you are looking to boost your students' learning, I highly recommend you read this book!

**Nicholas Soderstrom, PhD Instructor of Psychology
at Montana State University (@NickSoderstrom)**

When it comes to the idea of retrieval practice much has been written. As one of the most accessible areas of educational research, teachers have jumped at the chance to adopt it within their classroom practice. Within this book Kate develops and expands her discussion of practical strategies for effective retrieval practice, ensure that staff not only know what it is and how it works, but also how to go about applying it within classroom practice. From discussing the latest education research and sharing case studies of teachers and leaders implementing retrieval practice within their schools, this book provides a one-stop-shop for those that want to know about retrieval practice. A highly recommended read for all teachers.

**Nimish Lad, Curriculum and Research Leader at the Creative
Education Trust and Vice Principal of Wrenn School (@nlad84)**

This book really does delve into the inner workings of retrieval practice, moving teachers from a straightforward understanding of the theory which underpins the approach, to developing a deepened grasp of exactly why retrieval practice needs to feature in all of our schools. Immersed in the most recent research, working examples of what works and new insights backed by an incredible bibliography, Kate provides a piece of literature which will ensure that the quality of teaching not only secures success for our students, but fulfils us as evidence-informed professionals.

**Kat Howard, Assistant Principal at The Duston School
and author of *Stop Talking About Wellbeing*
and *Symbiosis: The Curriculum and the Classroom* (@SaysMiss)**

Whether you are a teacher who's unsure how to bring retrieval practice into your instruction, a school leader seeking to make retrieval practice happen more widely and effectively throughout your building, or an educator still building your understanding of retrieval practice, Kate Jones' *Retrieval Practice 2* is the perfect book for you. In this highly readable and timely volume (it features a chapter on pandemic-era education), Jones and a wide-ranging cast of teachers, leaders and researchers provide all the practical pointers, models, and cautions you will need to make retrieval practice a regular part of your teaching and learning.

Eric Kalenze, educator, researchED US organiser and author of *Education is Upside-Down* **and** *What the Academy Taught Us* **(@erickalenze)**

Retrieval practice is much more than the latest fad and Kate's first book *Retrieval Practice: Research & Resources for every classroom* shone a light on the vast research behind it and provided teachers like me with a wide variety of easy-to-use resources. In this sequel, Kate closes the gap between academia and our classrooms even more as she explores the most recent research on retrieval practice and discusses the common misconceptions when implementing this practice. Threaded through the book are case studies from classroom teachers alongside advice and guidance from some of the most eminent professors studying how we learn which really brings it to life. The book is brilliant and I read it so quickly; the case studies, what the researchers say and the Kirschner effect are my particular highlights. Retrieval practice works and this book is your toolkit to taking the next step in fully embedding it in your practice.

Darren Leslie, Principal Teacher of Learning & Teaching at Bell Baxter High School, Scotland and creator and host of the 'Becoming Educated' podcast (@dnleslie)

Retrieval Practice 2 is a fantastic follow on from Kate's first book. She takes strategies and research a step further going more in depth with more fabulous case studies. A brilliant and very valuable read. I cannot wait to start implementing in my classroom!

Alexandra Gordon, chemistry teacher in the Netherlands (@pedagogygeek)

In *Retrieval Practice 2*, Kate Jones has personally curated heavyweight research, the latest thinking and insights around this important learning strategy. She has distilled it to make it accessible and relevant. Crucially, this is not an academic compendium. Throughout, Kate draws on her own wealth of experience and expertise, as well as case studies of other retrieval advocates and pioneers, to bring the application to life. While it clearly bridges the gap between academia and the classroom, it would be wrong to think this is only for teachers. I talk to a lot of parents who want to support their teens and this is for them too. Thinking more broadly about how we can encourage our young people to study more effectively: *Retrieval Practice 2* is as practical and instructive as it is thought-provoking and interesting.

Nathan McGurl, Founder of thestudybuddy.com
which aims to helps students and parents with revision
and host of 'The Study Buddy' podcast (@nathanmcgurl)

Kate's first book on retrieval practice equipped me with strategies to implement it in my own classroom. *Retrieval Practice 2* has equipped me with ways to incorporate retrieval practice as a middle leader so that its use and impact is consistent and continually effective. I am now thinking of various systems to enable retrieval practice to land well within different classrooms so that there is a sustained impact. *Retrieval Practice 2* has opened my eyes to new dimensions of its benefits, due to its case studies from different educational teachers and leaders as well as research into how useful retrieval practice is for different types of students (SEND/gender). This is truly a revolutionary book.

Emily Folorunsho, head of history,
SLE and Lead Practitioner (@MissFolorunsho)

In *Retrieval Practice 2*, Kate Jones cements her place as the foremost authority in the application of retrieval practice within the classroom. *Retrieval Practice 2* is a meticulously considered insight into the application of retrieval practice across a number of classroom disciplines, drawing both on research and real life experiences. Kate manages to untangle some of the myths and misconceptions around retrieval practice while demonstrating how important and effective it is for children of all ages. Given the uncertain times in which this book was written, it is particularly pertinent to dedicate a chapter to utilise the methods during a pandemic. I cannot recommend this book more highly.

Ben Rothwell, Deputy Headteacher of
Victory Heights Primary School, Dubai (@VHPS_AsstHead)

CONTENTS

Foreword by Bradley Busch and Edward Watson   11

Introduction   13

Chapter 1: What does the latest research tell us about retrieval practice?   19

Chapter 2: Common mistakes with retrieval practice and how to avoid them   77

Chapter 3: Retrieval practice during a global pandemic   117

Chapter 4: Retrieval practice within each subject domain   147

FOREWORD

BY BRADLEY BUSCH AND EDWARD WATSON

Attempting a sequel after scaling the dizzy heights of success is a tricky thing to do. Chesney Hawkes, Peter Andre and B*Witched infamously fell short after their one-hit wonders. Fortunately, what Kate Jones has managed with *Retrieval Practice 2* is more akin to what *The Godfather II*, *Paddington 2* and *The Dark Knight* did in the cinematic world where the sequel is somehow even better than the original. This is no mean feat given that this book's predecessor is one of the best education books we have ever read. By now, many may well be familiar with the concept of retrieval practice – that is, generating an answer to a question helps students remember that information for longer. However, in the rush to embrace research, sometimes the message that underpins it can be morphed into something that it was not intended to be. With retrieval practice, some have described it as a call for more testing or a return to rote learning, neither of which is the case.

In an age of schools and teachers striving to be as evidence-informed as possible, finding a one-stop-shop that gives a thorough overview of the existing research in a particular area is much needed. However, it is not enough to just know, as a profession we must *do*. Where this book thrives is in looking at how to best apply the concepts of retrieval practice to students of different ages, in different subjects and different contexts. This includes the ever-growing importance of what retrieval practice looks like in an online learning environment. What *Retrieval Practice 2* does is clarify common myths and misconceptions and crucially highlights the many ways in which it can be woven into daily practice. From a personal perspective, we think the suggestions and tips around multiple-choice quizzes are the sort of thing that can be applied immediately with minimum effort which will yield significant returns.

Interwoven within the book are overviews of the seminal studies, practical suggestions, case studies as well as opinions and thoughts from eminent teachers, researchers and authors. This helps paint a full and rich picture, complete with nuance and context at the heart of it.

As such, there is something for everyone and probably everything for someone. This is supported by the way the book principally looks at retrieval practice but also broadens out to look at the wider areas surrounding teaching, learning and memory. This includes spacing, interleaving, desirable difficulties, pre-questions, homework and flashcards.

Plato once wrote that 'I am the wisest man alive, for I know one thing, and that is I know nothing.' Reading Kate's *Retrieval Practice 2* reminded us of this quote, as despite reading and writing extensively about retrieval practice in our own work, it is eye-opening to see just how much depth and subtlety exists when it comes to learning about how best to implement the research behind it. We do not doubt that no matter what a person's experience in the classroom or knowledge of the research, there are so many gems to glean from this book that we will all be better and more informed practitioners as a result.

In the spirit of retrieval practice, we thought we would sign off this foreword with a multiple-choice quiz.*

Kate Jones' latest book *Retrieval Practice 2* is:

a. Brilliantly written

b. Research-based

c. Thought-provoking

d. Easy to apply

e. All of the above

*You can find out towards the end of chapter 1 in this book why, ironically, this is not the best way to write a multiple-choice question. The correct answer is of course 'All of the above'.

Bradley Busch and Edward Watson are authors of *The Science of Learning 77 Studies That Every Teacher Needs to Know* and founders of Innerdrive.co.uk

INTRODUCTION

This book is written and intended to be a sequel to my previous book, *Retrieval Practice: Research & Resources for every classroom* and so I have assumed that if you have picked up this book then you already have background knowledge and understanding of retrieval practice. In summary, retrieval practice refers to the act of recalling information from memory without (or with minimal) support. As Professor Robert Bjork (Gocognitive, 2012) explains: 'When information is successfully retrieved from memory, its representation in memory is changed such that it becomes more recallable in the future', or more simply put by Bjork, 'Using our memory, shapes our memory'.

There has been a lot of explanation and discussion of working and long-term memory with the multi-store model of memory as well as the encoding, storage and retrieval process. This can be found in many books and blogs, including my own. This understanding of retrieval practice is now becoming part of the culture and language of learning in many schools which means the time to take the next steps of implementing, embedding and reflecting on retrieval practice in the classroom is now.

To refresh, information goes through various stages when it comes to memory. Beginning with the attention and encoding stages, students must pay attention and invest time and effort into committing information to memory. This information will be held in short-term memory initially, this later became known as – and is more widely referred to now – as the working memory. Baddeley and Hitch (1974) felt the concept of short-term memory, which features as part of the 'multi-store model of memory', was too simplistic and didn't fully grasp the complexities of what they referred to as working memory. Working and short-term memory both refer to an immediate type of memory that is limited both in terms of duration and capacity. Peterson and Peterson (1959) investigated the duration of working memory and various factors that cause working memory to decay. They concluded that all information stored in short-term memory which is not rehearsed will be lost within 18–30 seconds, although this will vary with individuals. Miller (1956) refers to how many items can be stored in short-term memory as 'magic number 7'. He suggested most adults can store seven items in short-term memory, plus or minus two. This means that it can range from 5 to 9 items, depending on the working memory capacity of different individuals.

In contrast, there is long-term memory. In terms of capacity and duration, long-term memory is incredibly powerful and we do not know its actual limitations. However, just because information has been transferred to long-term memory does not mean it is automatically retrievable. Professors Robert Bjork and Elizabeth Bjork have explored this thoroughly with 'the new theory of disuse' (1992). They write: 'To say that we have an impressive capacity to store information in memory is a gross understatement [...] Conversely, to say that we can always retrieve our memories is a gross overstatement.' How easily information can be retrieved will largely depend on two factors: storage strength and retrieval strength. Storage strength refers to how deeply embedded and secure memories are in long-term memory. Retrieval strength refers to how retrievable memories are; how easily and quickly they can be accessed. If you would like a more in-depth recap of how memory works and how it can impact teaching and learning you can find articles on my website (lovetoteach87.com) or you can complete a free online course I created with Seneca Learn about retrieval practice. A certificate is awarded on completion and access to this can be found at the back of this book with a QR code or by visiting senecalearning.com

This book is deliberately different from my previous in a variety of ways. The main and noticeable difference readers will observe is that this book does not focus on sharing lesson ideas and resource templates, although there are practical examples throughout. The reason for this is due to the volume of ideas and activities included in my previous book. I believe there's more than enough to provide teachers with a solid bank of retrieval activities to trial, adapt or simply download and use in the classroom. It is important to have concrete examples to use in the classroom and that was one of my priorities with my previous book. You can access all the free templates from my previous book by scanning the QR code at the back of this book to my TES resources page.

As important as classroom examples are, we do not need to keep reinventing the wheel in regards to task design but instead **implement, embed** and **reflect**. This book will focus on key aspects linked to retrieval practice including findings from the latest academic research and reflections from my own experiences, as well as other classroom practitioners and school leaders. Every educational book should bring something new to the table and have something different to offer teachers. I aim to do that with this book, although I am well aware readers will have varying degrees of knowledge and understanding when it comes to retrieval practice and it can be difficult to pitch at the right level. This is my third book and when I write a book I write the book that I, as a teacher, would want to read with the hope I can continue to improve my practice and grow in confidence. I hope others in education will find what I write both interesting and useful.

In hindsight, after the publication of my previous book I felt there were some areas linked to retrieval practice I wished I had included or discussed in more depth but I was keen to keep the book concise. I now have the opportunity to explore more areas that I haven't previously. In my previous book, there was a range of case studies and resources from across a range of subjects but there was a noticeable lack of discussion and examples from practical subjects such as PE, art and music. This can even be viewed as propagating the myth that retrieval practice is not suitable for those subjects when in fact it is. I have been able to include examples from those subjects in this book.

In the last 12 months, I have worked with many teachers. These include my own colleagues and educators online and I have delivered training focused on retrieval practice to schools around the world. This professional development training has varied from keynote presentations to workshops and live 'question and answer' sessions. These discussions and sessions have been thought-provoking and insightful for me. It is clear leaders and teachers are keen to embrace and embed retrieval practice. It has been fascinating to see where different schools are at in their journey and progression with retrieval practice. I want to express my gratitude and appreciation to all of the educators I have spoken to about retrieval practice as it has influenced my own practice, led to further research and consideration, as well as contributing to this book.

Despite writing two books, a range of educational blogs and speaking at various teaching events, I have never directly engaged with academic researchers until now. I reached out to academics and cognitive scientists, whose published findings and writings I have been reading and following for many years. To my delight, their responses were very encouraging as well as incredibly insightful. Leading names in the field of retrieval practice such as Professor Henry Roediger, Professors Robert Bjork and Elizabeth Bjork, Dylan Wiliam and more are all featured in this book, offering their unique and exclusive advice for teachers on what we should know about the application of retrieval practice in our classrooms. I hope you find this as exciting to read as I did.

So, in regards to retrieval practice where are we now? This is an important question to consider. The research about retrieval practice continues to be carried out and I think it is a very exciting time in education as we can delve deeper into the benefits and potential pitfalls of this strategy. The research continues to be positively overwhelming; retrieval practice is an effective teaching and learning technique. It is time to move the conversation around retrieval practice forward.

As I mentioned, all schools are at their own unique point in their retrieval practice journey. I have worked with schools that have asked me to introduce and explain the basic components of retrieval practice and the cognitive psychology elements. Other schools, including the school I currently work at, have been using retrieval practice for many years now and are continually adapting and improving their approaches at a departmental and whole school level. They are often sharing best practice with other schools whilst still keen to learn more. I am delighted this book features two case studies from leaders that are leading the way, at a departmental and whole school level, with the implementation of retrieval practice in their schools. There are examples in this book from experts in their subject domains with advice and guidance about what retrieval practice looks like in each subject. This will be helpful for classroom teachers, heads of departments/faculties and senior leaders that manage a range of subjects outside of their specialism. Whatever stage you are at with retrieval practice I hope you find this book helpful in your journey.

2020 was undoubtedly a year of disruption due to the outbreak and spread of the pandemic. Education around the world has been dramatically impacted by the decision for many schools to deliver remote online learning and public examinations being cancelled. It could be tempting to consider putting retrieval practice on hold to catch up on the missed lesson time and instead focus on delivering as much new content as possible. This would be a mistake. Now, more than ever, we need to ensure students are using retrieval practice both inside and outside of lessons. Retrieval practice is a solution (not a single solution) to the interruption to learning from Covid-19. If schools have yet to fully embrace this strategy then now is the time to do so.

I have been asked before why I am so interested in retrieval practice and I can understand why someone would ask me this. Anyone who has seen my social media channels, who has read my teaching blogs and books or listened to me present will be aware of the enthusiasm I have when speaking or writing about retrieval practice. The reason for my curiosity, motivation and interest in this field is simply down to the positive impact it has on learning. I have fully embraced retrieval practice and urge all those around me to do so too, including colleagues, students and parents in the wider school community. Dylan Wiliam (Lock, 2020) has noted that 'the benefits of practice testing and distributed practice are two of the most strongly supported learning strategies in all of psychology'. Retrieval practice is so powerful that everyone should know about it, whether they are in school or not. I am keen to spread the word and keep the conversation alive. Retrieval practice is an effective and essential learning strategy.

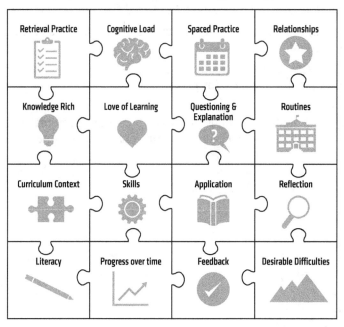

Despite my enthusiasm, I am aware of my own possible confirmation bias and there are limitations to this strategy. Retrieval practice alone does not provide all of the solutions and it isn't a silver bullet in education, but it is one of the strongest and sharpest tools in our teaching toolkit. The infographic of my teaching and learning puzzle was created to visually show that retrieval practice is only one piece of a complex puzzle when it comes to teaching and learning.

I deliberately created it as a jigsaw puzzle to emphasise how retrieval practice can be even more beneficial when combined with other factors such as spaced practice, effective feedback, classroom routines and more. These aspects are intertwined and connected to everything we do in the classroom. Retrieval practice is not another fad in education that will come and go. Retrieval practice will stand the test of time and rightly so.

References

Baddeley, A. D. and Hitch, G. (1974) 'Working memory'. In G. H. Bower (Ed.), *The psychology of learning and motivation: Advances in research and theory* (Vol. 8, pp. 47–89). New York: Academic Press.

Gocognitivie (2012) 'robert bjork - using our memory shapes our memory', YouTube [Online] 12 July. Retrieved from: www.bit.ly/39UOQYV

Lock, S. (Ed.) (2020) *The researchEd guide to Leadership*. Woodbridge: John Catt Educational.

Miller, G. A. (1956) 'The magical number seven, plus or minus two: some limits on our capacity for processing information', *Psychological Review* 63 (2) pp. 81-97.

Peterson, L. R. and Peterson, M. J. (1959) 'Short-term retention of individual verbal items', *Journal of Experimental Psychology* 58 pp. 193-198.

CHAPTER 1:
WHAT DOES THE LATEST RESEARCH TELL US ABOUT RETRIEVAL PRACTICE?

The research linked to memory and the 'testing effect'[1] dates back over a century with the most well-known being Ebbinghaus' forgetting curve in 1885. Through an experiment Hermann Ebbinghaus carried out on himself, he illustrated how memory rapidly declines over time unless the forgetting curve is interrupted. It has since been replicated many times to present similar findings and results. When I first began engaging with educational research I was shocked to discover a lot of the information and research that was new to me was not new at all. I found myself confused as to why this information had not reached teachers – this was information we all need to know. Senior leader and author of *Teaching Rebooted: Using the Science of Learning to Transform Classroom Practice*, Jon Tait refers to this as the hidden truths of learning. Tait asks why was this research and information hidden from teachers for so long? Academic researchers also asked this question too: why do teachers not know of this important information on learning? Thankfully, research is becoming more accessible and shared more widely amongst the teaching profession. The gap between the academic and teaching community is closing.

For this chapter, I have decided to focus predominantly on research linked to retrieval practice from the last five years, but there are still some references to research findings from more than five years ago. I also didn't want to repeat the discussion and exploration of research findings that I wrote about in my previous book. We must take an **evidence-informed** approach to teaching and learning rather than an **evidence-led** approach. Research is another piece of the complex teaching and learning puzzle, but only one piece of that puzzle.

---

1   Retrieval practice is essentially harnessing the testing effect.

Paul Kirschner is widely quoted in my writing as his work – ranging from research findings, books and blogs – has had a positive influence on my classroom practice. Kirschner and Tim Surma (2020) have dedicated an interesting discussion around the term evidence-informed pedagogy. They write: 'There is an, albeit sometimes subtle, distinction between evidence-based and evidence-informed in terms of practice in education', adding that 'an evidence-based practice is an approach to practice that focuses practitioner attention on sound empirical evidence in professional decision making and action'. Kirschner and Surma further explain: 'Evidence-informed practice is still based on empirical evidence, but acknowledges the fact that it's harder for real classroom practice to determine what works for who under which circumstances. What seems to work in one classroom does not always work in another classroom.' Absolutely. This is something as educators we are well aware of despite the approach to retrieval practice tending to be more generic as research has shown it is effective with learners of all ages and abilities.

Kirschner and Sumra point out: 'Five year olds are different from fifteen year olds both with respect to their cognitive development and their knowledge and expertise, a lesson on concepts and definitions is different from a lesson on applications, and to a lesser extent a lesson in chemistry differs from a lesson in drawing. Also, what works for one teacher might not work for another because teachers differ qualitatively; subtle and not so subtle differences between teachers mean that the way that they carry out the same thing differs both in how it is carried out and how it is perceived by their students. Also, what works in a lesson today won't necessarily work in the same lesson this afternoon, tomorrow, or in three months.' This touches upon some of the key differences affecting learners whilst not moving towards territory that all students learn differently with learning styles, which Kirschner and many other leading academics have debunked, to the relief of many teachers around the world (myself included).

Kirschner and Surma further explain: 'While "evidence-based" provides fairly hard results, "evidence-informed" is less hard, but still very useful with a higher chance of success if applied thoughtfully.' This is where the implementation, embedding and reflection aspects become so crucial. Taking an evidence-informed approach to teaching and learning must be at a whole-school level. It is simply not enough for a classroom teacher to be attempting to do so on their own, nor a small group of enthusiastic teachers working in collaboration in the corner of the staffroom. Being an evidence-informed school can be a factor that will influence teacher recruitment and retention. Many teachers are actively seeking positions as classroom teachers and leaders, in schools that adopt this approach. Along the same lines, schools that do not take an evidence-informed approach risk the retention of their staff who can choose to leave and move elsewhere. In September 2019 I joined a new school and I was asked during the interview: Why this school? Why do you want to work here? I had a wide range of reasons as to why I was so keen to secure this role. The fact the school very openly and proudly advocates an evidence-informed approach to teaching and learning was a significant one. I also felt quietly confident at the interview because I knew the school would be looking to appoint a teacher and leader that engages with evidence and research through professional learning to improve classroom practice, which I do.

Based on my personal experiences (and I know many other practitioners that feel the same) taking an evidence-informed approach to teaching and learning has significantly increased my motivation and confidence as a teacher. The ripple effect of this increased confidence as a teacher extends to working smarter instead of harder or longer. Adopting and embedding approaches that have a positive impact on my workload yet does not hinder learning. In addition to allowing more time to focus on other areas of professional development such as continually enhancing and deepening my subject knowledge. This has allowed me to work with colleagues and share good practice with others, either in my school context or outside of my school. An evidence-informed approach has led to me feeling consistently driven and motivated. I find myself always wanting to learn more and striving to do better instead of feeling discouraged, disheartened or burnt out. Finally, I have seen the improvements in terms of outcomes, results and confidence with the students that I teach as a result of experience and evidence improving my classroom practice. An evidence-informed approach is efficient and effective as well as thoroughly enjoyable. I refer to this passion and desire to become an evidence-informed teacher and an obligation to challenge outdated and debunked neuromyths as the 'Kirschner effect'.

I recall hearing a question posed by Dr Jared Cooney Horvath in 2018 and it has stayed with me since. It is often at the back of my mind when I hear discussions on evidence-informed or based practices in schools. Cooney Horvath said, 'Whenever I hear the term evidence-based practice, I always ask the same question: whose evidence do you mean?' This is a very pertinent question that we should be asking and be aware of when considering this approach in schools.

Frequently, it can feel as if everyone has an opinion as to how schools should be run and how teachers should teach. This could be since everyone has their own experiences with education but, by the same token, it's likely we have all been to visit a doctor yet the majority of us do not feel qualified to dish out medical advice! Cooney Horvath co-authored a marvellous book with David Bott which includes a chapter dedicated to the mistakes that can be made in terms of evidence and its application in schools. Cooney Horvath and Bott (2020) write, 'Nobody in the world understands the decisions teachers must make, the context within which they must make them, or the goals they are trying to achieve by making them. Nobody, that is, except for teachers themselves.' I can picture everyone reading this nodding along enthusiastically just as I did when I first read it.

Cooney Horvath and Bott further add: 'Only teachers have devoted the requisite time, effort and energy to the craft of teaching to effectively recognise and account for the emergent properties that exist within a classroom. Simply put, in order for laboratory research to drive educational practice, prescriptive translation must be undertaken by the only people qualified to do it: teachers. Don't get me wrong – none of this is to suggest that brain or behavioural research is useless. On the contrary, this work can and often does supply teachers with powerful concepts to draw upon for inspiration and ideas. However, the ultimate determination of what these concepts mean for teaching practice can only be derived and established by the practitioners of that craft.' This message is reassuring for teachers, not only does it address the complexities of teaching – as did the writings of Kirschner and Surma – but it recognises the importance of teacher autonomy and professional judgement in the implementation of academic research. It is one thing engaging with and understanding academic research but it is another to apply it in a classroom. Fortunately, retrieval practice is an area of research that, although in many respects can be considered complex, can be implemented and embedded into classroom practice with relative ease. This is partly because quizzing and testing have long since been established in schools but the focus has shifted from testing as a form of assessment to regular low stakes testing to improve learning and memory.

Daniel Willingham was asked as part of his popular series in the *American Educator*: 'Should Teachers Know the Basic Science of How Children Learn?' Willingham stated (2019): 'There's no doubt that research bearing directly on classroom practice is crucial.' He goes on to explain the key differences between what researchers call 'basic science' and 'applied science'. Basic science refers to 'research that is conducted not with the aim of improving education, but with the aim of providing a scientific description of the world' in comparison to applied science which can influence education through the use of scientific methods to 'evaluate the effectiveness of different educational practices and suggest new ideas for instructional methods'. Willingham does also recognise that despite educational research being incredibly important, 'Scientific findings provide one (but obviously not the only) source of information contributing to educators' beliefs about the nature of children.' This is the sensible approach to take, combining the research, evidence and findings with our own classroom experiences and contexts.

An issue we face as educators, as observed by Willingham (2019), 'is that basic science represents a moving target, researchers keep learning more! How can you keep up? One substantial problem is evaluating the quality of the resources you encounter on the web, in books, in professional development sessions, and so on.' It may seem overwhelming at times to keep up with the pace of change but we must take our time to carefully consider any alterations made to our classroom practice. Teachers have confided in me that they can feel intimidated or foolish for not always being aware of the latest research. It is difficult and no one should be made to feel inferior because they haven't read X amount of books or journals. Professional development is something I explore later in this chapter and it is an area where both schools and individual teachers need to take responsibility. Schools should not expect their teachers to be engaging in professional development without offering any form of support, which should be provided in terms of time, resources and funding. Similarly, teachers should not just rely on their schools to deliver professional development, especially as there is a wealth of high-quality professional learning materials available online, at our fingertips, ready to access. Explicitly linked to the point Willingham made about basic science being a moving target, in terms of the latest developments with academic research and retrieval practice, the rest of this chapter poses the question: What does the research tell us about...?

Retrieval practice in a classroom setting?

Dylan Wiliam (2017a) has been widely quoted as saying, 'what is interesting is not what works in education, but under what circumstances does it work?' We know that context is key. A lot of the academic research published about retrieval practice comes from experiments and tests carried out in universities in North America. This does not discredit the research but it does make us ask the questions of 'Does this apply to a classroom context?' and 'What does this look like in my classroom?' This is important because we are teaching and students are learning in conditions different to the ones in the research we are engaging with.

Dr Cindy Nebel has written about the various problems researchers face when attempting to carry out research, experiments and studies in classrooms. Nebel (2017) writes that 'classrooms are messy research venues. There are numerous variables that we have no control over. We cannot control the motivation level of the students. In a laboratory, the students have somewhat equal motivation levels – their scores do not in any way affect whether or not they will receive credit for participating.' Nebel further adds that 'when we move outside the laboratory we also have to consider that students are engaged with material outside of class. We might find that similar classes cause interference or confusion with what we are teaching (leading to a decrease in retention) while other classes may cause elaboration (leading to an increase in retention). Younger students in particular may have differences in the quality of help they get from their parents. And we haven't even begun to talk about differences in teachers.' This really does highlight that carrying out research is complex in itself and even more so in a classroom environment. I have been guilty of not realising the sheer volume of time, effort, design, considerations and processes that take place for each research study and experiment to take place and reach publication.

There are some reservations towards academic research within the teaching community. One reason could be the conditions in which the research is carried out which vary significantly to our own classroom context. It is important academic researchers recognise key differences but educators should also appreciate and understand the reasons why a controlled environment is often much easier to conduct research in. Nebel summarises this well, 'In short, applied research is hard. All of these variables mean that any given manipulation is considerably less likely to work in the classroom setting than it is in the laboratory (where many of these factors are controlled). Despite the majority of the research conducted in this setting, there have been studies conducted in classroom contexts too and this continues to take place. This includes studies by Carpenter, Pashler and Cepeda (2009) and McDaniel, Wildman and Anderson (2012) amongst many more.

Moreira, Pinto, Starling and Jaeger (2019) published 'Retrieval Practice in Classroom Settings: A Review of Applied Research' which recognised an overwhelming amount of research, demonstrating that: 'Typically, practising retrieval yields significantly greater long-term retention of the studied materials than just restudying them', but noted that in 'educational settings, however, the format of these tests are often different'. The review summarised the main differences between a laboratory and classroom context. Those differences included: the amount of information students are often required to learn, the motivation to learn and engage with materials[2], the way the new content is presented, and 'more importantly, the differences in the amount of distraction existing in each of these environments.' This links back to the observations made by Nebel.

The main questions posed in the meta-analytic review were the following:

1. Is the testing effect replicable in educational settings?

2. Are there types of tests that are more (or less) beneficial than others in educational contexts?

3. Are the potential benefits of retrieval practice more prominent to specific age ranges in educational settings?

4. Does retrieval practice remain beneficial when compared to 'stronger' control conditions in the classroom?

5. Does corrective feedback enhance the benefits of retrieval practice in classroom settings?

6. Based on the answers for the questions above, is the current applied literature substantial enough to instil the recommendation of retrieval practice in school environments?

The review also stated 'even though retrieval practice emerges as a promising strategy to improve learning in classroom environments, there is not enough evidence available at this moment to determine whether it is as beneficial as alternative learning activities frequently adopted in classroom settings.' This quote must be read carefully. It's not suggesting teachers should not use retrieval practice, the conclusion that follows is very encouraging and positive in terms of retrieval in the classroom, but this article is pointing out that further research is required (in terms of the questions posed and the success and impact of the testing effect) in classroom environments, rather than laboratory conditions.

---

2   We are very aware of the different levels of motivation within our classes and the children we work with.

The review also commented 'an important question for both laboratory and classroom research, is whether these different types of tests are differently effective in eliciting testing effects.'

The conclusion of the research review stated: 'The reviewed articles show that testing effects can be in general successfully reproduced in classroom settings, with typical classroom materials and although considerable work should be done to elucidate these issues, the reviewed studies show that retrieval practice in the form of multiple-choice and fill-in-the-gaps tests are a promising learning strategy to be used in classroom settings.' More research and review regarding the questions asked is required and no doubt further study into retrieval practice in classroom settings would certainly be welcomed and prove to be useful.

The pre-questioning effect?

We know retrieval practice focuses on testing students on material they have already learned and that it is better to do so once some time has passed and forgetting has occurred to make it more effortful and effective. There have been various studies and experiments carried out to investigate if giving students pre-questions (questions about lesson content before they have been exposed to that material) supports learning. Based on the various studies I have encountered, the results replicated are generally similar, suggesting students that have answered pre-questions prior to material who then answer the same questions after exposure to the material, will perform better than those students who did not receive the questions beforehand. Bjork and Bjork (2012) have studied the pre-questioning effect and concluded pretests appear to be beneficial for subsequent learning. This has very powerful and important implications for the classroom as it suggests giving students pre-questions will enhance memory and learning.

The main type of experiment carried out with pre-questioning tends to focus on students randomly allocated to two different groups: a pre-question group and a control group. Research has been undertaken with various forms of questioning from open-ended free recall and fill in the blanks but mainly multiple-choice questions. The pre-question group will be asked a set of questions in advance and will then be asked the same pre-questions in addition to new questions after engaging with the study material. The control group will not see the questions before the lesson but will answer all of the questions afterwards. Some studies have included a post-question group, where they have only been asked questions after a period of time has passed instead of before or immediately after the lesson material has been delivered.

Carpenter, Rahman and Perkins (2017) wanted to investigate if the previous research findings from laboratories around pre questions would be replicated when using pre-questions in a classroom setting. The abstract stated that 'results from this experiment showed that within the pre-questioned group students did better on pre-questioned material than on non-pre-questioned material, replicating various findings on the effects of pre-questions. Additionally, there was no difference in the learning of non-pre-questioned material between the pre-question group and control group. On a delayed retention test students (both in the pre question and control group) did better on questions they saw before (on the end of class quiz) compared to questions they did not see before.' It was a compelling read and this paper would encourage us as teachers to promote the use of pre-questions in our lessons.

Studies linked to pre-questions have varied from focusing on reading texts to in-class quizzing. Carpenter and Toftness (2017) conducted research using pre-questioning as a strategy to support learning and retrieval practice with video lectures, using a pre-question group and a control group. In the pre-question group, students answered questions before watching an educational video and, naturally, found this was very difficult. This resorted to guesswork and resulted in less than 5% accuracy, replicating previous findings. The control group were not asked any questions before viewing the video. Both groups were later asked questions, immediately after viewing the video[3] and the questions asked consisted of some of the pre-questions that the first group had seen in addition to questions that were new to both groups. The results from this video experiment showed that the sample of students from the pre-question group did perform better in the final test than the control group. The pre-question group performed 15% higher answering the pre-questions in comparison to answering the new questions that they had not seen before. In terms of the new and unseen questions after the video, the pre-question group achieved 12% higher than the control group. Overall, the pre-question group performed 19% better than the control group who did not see any questions before the video, suggesting that when using video content it would be useful to show students the pre-questions in advance.

---

3   A critique could be that this did not allow time for forgetting to occur.

Pre-questions can provide students with insight into the content and material they will be engaging with during the lesson, this can spark their interest and curiosity as well as potentially increase their effort and focus. Retrieval practice, unlike other forms of study, such as re-reading and highlighting, does not give students a false sense of confidence. Students can sometimes assume they already know the answers but the pre-questions can explicitly show them that they do not, therefore they need to pay attention. The pre-question effect could counteract the Dunning–Kruger effect. However, there can be possible negative implications for learning with the pre-question effect and this is where I have read slightly conflicting research. Carpenter, Rahman and Perkins (2017) stated the findings showed pre-questions can improve learning of the pre-questioned material without affecting the learning of non-pre-questioned material. However, there is evidence to suggest otherwise. When students have been exposed to pre-questions before exposure to lesson material, this may encourage them to focus and direct their attention solely on the material linked to the pre-questions. This isn't necessarily a bad thing, but the issue is what about the rest of the lesson material that didn't feature in the pre-questions? Students may neglect content that was not pre-questioned but is still of importance and value to learning.

Bradley Busch advised that pre-questioning works best with the teacher in a classroom rather than as a self-study strategy (obviously students cannot create questions before they view material and at the study/revision stage students should not be engaging with completely new material anyway). Busch (2017) wrote in an article: 'It's worth noting that this benefit is mostly felt when the teacher controls the pace of the learning. When it is self-directed by pupils, the effect may be lessened' adding 'to make sure you're maximising their effect, maybe use pre-questions in lessons based on videos or PowerPoint presentations so you can control the pace.' He recommends that using pre-questions is a great way to start a lesson.

Is this something you and your colleagues already do? Pre-questioning is not a technique I use consistently but I have been trialling and implementing it in my lessons and I have found that students respond well to it. One student told me they felt this technique helped their concentration and wished this was used more widely in lessons. Pre-questions with a textbook or reading material can prompt students to skim read and simply search for the answers rather than get to grips with the rest of the text. To ensure non-pre-questioned material is not ignored, the material can be regularly tested in following retrieval sessions. Altogether, it does appear to be a useful strategy to promote learning and retrieval practice, we just need to consider the implications of the non-pre-questioned material and ensure that it is not neglected.

Retrieval practice and gender differences?

A lot of research cites that retrieval practice is an effective strategy for all students regardless of age and gender and the work of Professor John Dunlosky *et al* (2013) is a key example. I have not encountered any research that suggests there are cognitive differences between male and female learners, therefore retrieval practice is a strategy to be promoted with all students regardless of their gender. I previously worked in an independent school in Abu Dhabi where the boys and girls were taught on the same school site but in different buildings in segregated classes.[4] This opened my eyes to many gender differences and behaviours as the buildings were exactly the same in their design but what was happening in each of the buildings was very different. There were similarities but also some stark contrasts in terms of behaviour, motivation and effort. Teachers and leaders have often asked me for advice as to how they can encourage more boys to embrace retrieval practice. There have long been issues in education with an academic gender gap and the best summary I have read of the issues facing this gap is taken from the brilliant and powerful book *Boys Don't Try? Rethinking Masculinity in Schools* by Matt Pinkett and Mark Roberts.

Pinkett and Roberts (2019) summarise the problems linked with boys: 'Boys underperform at all key stages of primary and secondary education compared to girls. Boys are more likely to be excluded from school. Boys are less likely to go to university; boys are less likely to find paid work between the ages 22 and 29. And when these boys become young men, they are three times more likely than women to be victims of suicide. They also belong to the gender that makes up 96% of the UK prison population.' Shocking statistics. It's no wonder teachers and leaders in schools are desperately searching for strategies to change this narrative and find solutions to narrow – or, even better, close – the gender gap. I certainly will not claim retrieval practice can do so, as it is very complex. Pinkett and Roberts address and tackle common myths about boys in schools. They offer advice and possible

---

4   This meant a lot of running from building to building between lessons but that was an entirely different challenge!

solutions to be applied in the classroom. To explore this topic about retrieval practice and gender I contacted Pinkett and Roberts. I asked if they were aware of any research concerning retrieval practice and gender. They knew there was little research in this specific field but I was directed to a research article published in 2018, by Mathieu Gagnon and Stephanie Cormier. Gagnon and Cormier (2018) comment on the previous studies: 'To date, however, this research has focused exclusively on Americans and has paid little attention to potential gender differences. The present study addressed such limits by using a web-based survey of the rereading, self-testing, and distributed learning habits of 1371 French-speaking Canadian undergraduates.' They found that 'residual analyses suggest that females are more likely to engage in distributed learning than their male counterparts'. Overall, the findings conclude girls are more likely to use retrieval and spaced practice than boys and so we need to make sure we are encouraging boys to use retrieval practice independently. In terms of gender and retrieval practice, there are no differences cognitively but there are with attitude and approach.

In his book *The Boy Question*, Mark Roberts argues that boys are more likely to stop using effective study strategies, even if they are aware of the benefits because they leave revision too late. This then becomes more of an organisation issue because if boys do not start revision early they will not be able to carry out spaced retrieval practice and will have to resort to cramming and ineffective techniques. I think this is very important for classroom teachers and leaders to be aware of so we can try to support male learners with their planning and preparation. The gender gap has also been described as a confidence gap. There have been various research studies that have looked into the differences between confidence and gender (both in an educational setting and the adult workplace too). A study by Cho (2017) explained: 'The findings highlight that female students are not less confident than male students, but they are rather less overconfident.'

Is there a connection with the gender and confidence gap linking to study strategies? Is it possible boys are not embracing effective study strategies as they can overestimate their abilities and perhaps, in contrast, girls will use these study strategies sooner because they lack confidence? I appreciate the complexities of gender and we need to be careful not to make sweeping statements but the research can provide us with some valuable insight to support our teachers and allow us to consider what interventions we can put into place. Do the research findings on gender and retrieval and spaced practice ring true for you based on your classroom experiences? I can recall a male member of my tutor group that was bitterly disappointed with his result in a mock examination as he had not achieved the grade he had hoped for. He insisted he had revised and failed to understand his low grade. I asked him how he had revised and he told me he carried out lots of re-reading the night before the exam, as I have heard time and time before, even though I had continually stressed the importance of retrieval and spaced practice. He argued that any revision is better than no revision (this is true but a weak argument) and he felt that re-reading before the exam was enough and he deserved a pat on the back for doing so. It was also much easier for him to re-read than self-test. Self-testing requires more effort, energy and motivation because re-reading gave him a false sense of confidence in his abilities despite the fact re-reading does not tell you what you can or cannot recall.

I do not think this is an issue specific to gender but, from my own experiences, I have found girls generally – not always, of course – to be more receptive to retrieval practice. The different attitudes towards effective study strategies are something I will be more aware and mindful of in the future.

Implementing retrieval practice through leadership at all levels?

Teachers and leaders at all levels in a school need to be getting to grips with retrieval practice but how this strategy is implemented and embedded will ultimately be impacted by the leadership across a school. The principal of The Duston School, Samuel Strickland writes in his superb book *Education Exposed 2* that, 'Leadership is not a race. Deep-rooted change takes time: improvements must be fully understood, firmly embedded and key systems and routines have to become habitual.' A very important message that can be applied to teaching and learning across a school, especially the idea of deep-rooted change in learning habits and routines when it comes to implementing and embedding retrieval practice.

Dylan Wiliam (Lock, 2020) has stated that 'in terms of practical steps, perhaps the first thing to do is to make sure that teachers are aware of the research on the power of practice testing and distributed practice while making it clear that how these ideas are implemented in practice will require a considerable amount of professional judgement'. In terms of implementation, this is what we must ensure – a combination of an experience and evidence-informed approach with professional judgement. Leaders at all levels really do need to be on board with the process of implementing, embedding and reflecting on the use of retrieval practice. Leaders that are still in the classroom will need to lead by example using this in their practice. Leaders at all levels should be taking an active role to engage with evidence linked to retrieval practice then share this with their teams. Leaders can be looking as to how teachers are implementing and embedding regular retrieval into their classroom practice but, as always, this should be supportive and developmental rather than judgemental.

Hugh Richards is a chartered teacher of history and subject leader at Huntington School in York. Hugh is also programme leader on the Historical Association's Subject Leadership course. I attended an excellent webinar Hugh delivered on applying the findings of cognitive psychology to teaching and learning within history. This was the first time I had engaged with professional development linked to cognitive psychology but also specifically in the context of the subject I teach and lead at a departmental level and I had found the webinar very interesting and helpful. There has been some discussion of cognitive psychology and its application to the subject of history but I believe much more collaboration and reflection around cognitive psychology and individual subjects across the curriculum is now required. In this case study, Hugh shares how he has embedded retrieval practice into his subject domain as both a teacher and middle leader.

How we went about implementing retrieval practice in the department at Huntington School
Hugh Richards

1. We decided where to concentrate our efforts.

Huntington has been an EEF Research School since 2016. As subject leader, my role is to blend evidence-informed 'best bets' with the proven traditions and evolving practice of the history teaching community. Generally speaking, we look at incorporating evidence-based strategies when established history teaching traditions and wisdom hasn't quite had the effect we want. In the case of disciplined retrieval practice, the driving factor was the huge content demands of the 2016 GCSE and the consequential impact on our most vulnerable learners. The evidence was clearly in favour of implementing systematic retrieval practice to help GCSE students from across the ability range to navigate this increased demand.

2. We tried to anticipate problems with blending a generic strategy into our subject.

As a subject leader, I always ensure we pause and think carefully before adopting a new generic element into our teaching. As this is a process that can only be done by the subject experts in a school I think subject leaders play a key role at this stage.

Problem 1: What exactly do students need to retrieve?

We initially underestimated the importance of identifying the really core knowledge we wanted students to retrieve. We also underestimated the time and effort needed for this process.
We found lesson time invested in retrieval was pointless if that knowledge was relatively niche or highly specific. Whilst history teaching and textbooks rightly blend the core knowledge with useful and engaging illustrative detail even the highest-achieving students need not remember all of this. For example, in the table that follows question one requires knowledge of a single fact that is of limited use however, question two requires students to marshal far more knowledge, as well as to consider a cause and effect process:

Question 1	Question 2
When was the second major Public Health Act of the industrial period?	Which of these helps explain the improvement of public health in the later Industrial period?
A. 1846 B. 1856 C. 1875 D. 1911	A. Widespread deaths from cholera epidemics B. Establishment of the NHS C. Working-class men being able to vote D. The discovery of the 'germ theory of disease'

Indeed focusing retrieval tasks on specific information, such as in question 1 above, can cause further problems. If an essay question allows a student to use any 20 pieces of information from a total of 50 valid examples they have encountered in class, focusing retrieval on 20 narrow specifics undermines confidence and engenders confusion. A student might be able to happily retrieve most of the remaining 30 facts and should have the chance to consolidate this, as it still could be deployed to gain full marks in the essay. This exaggerated extreme is highly unlikely, but the possibility of it highlights an issue for application in history.

Problem 2: How can the practice reflect the kind of retrieval they need in history?

Compared to many subjects, history assessments offer few memory prompts to students. In a typical essay question, students get a single sentence question that identifies a topic. They are left to use their knowledge to establish the scope of the question and identify what should and should not be included from a wide range of information that could be connected to the topic. This extended response requires quite a different type of retrieval to a series of one-mark recall questions, largely because there is a process of categorisation and selection needed as students marshal their knowledge into a paragraph structure that addresses the question.

Problem 3: There is no way to make interleaved teaching make sense in history.

For some subjects, there is an option of interleaving topics to benefit retrieval practice. In history, this is entirely undesirable. History is a carefully sequenced and chronologically organised narrative. Starting one GCSE unit, then starting a second, then starting a third, fourth and fifth before returning to the second part of the first unit runs counter to tried and tested traditions in history teaching. Therefore, we decided that, in history, interleaving and distribution more or less has to be confined to short retrieval tasks at the start of lessons.

3. Our key conclusion was that time invested in planning retrieval tasks would pay off later.

Successful implementation of a piece of work on this scale – distributed retrieval practice tasks targeted on core content across a GCSE course – takes real thinking about. At all levels of the school, we use a simple Venn diagram to guide decision making. Good decisions at Huntington are those that fit the centre of this diagram.

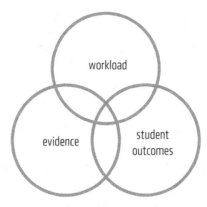

Retrieval practice passes the evidence and outcomes tests comfortably. The workload element was critical. Retrieval in history that allows students to select from a wider knowledge base has the potential to result in a great deal of extra planning and/or marking, especially if it is to double as a useful formative assessment. This was where the heart of the leadership issue lay.

It rapidly became apparent there was an inverse relationship between time committed to planning retrieval tasks and the time needed to run them in lessons. We were looking for tasks that were both time-efficient at the start of the lesson and didn't result in increased planning or marking load for the teacher. Achieving both turned out to be really tricky. For example, a really well-tuned multiple choice question like question 2 saves time in lessons as it is quick to deliver and mark, but takes a comparatively long time to plan. Tasks that reflect the needs of the history assessment (the essay question problem discussed) generally take longer to mark, as they are open-ended and thus peer marking gets bogged down with students needing to repeatedly check the validity of a diverse range of examples.

4. Therefore, our process of implementation looked something like this:

We made it our single major focus for a whole year.

■ As subject leader, I devoted the maximum possible meeting, CPD and curriculum development time to this project.

■ Training on how to approach the tasks was given before commencing the next stage.

- It was clear that the time would be needed for resource creation, so I planned accordingly. About 85% of the CPD and meeting time dedicated to this was teachers collaboratively planning well-thought-out classroom resources.

Following the recommendations of Richard Kennett, we drafted and edited tightly-focused core content documents:

- Each hundred-page textbook down to just five pages of bullet points.
- Investing significant time allowed us to focus retrieval tasks on the information that would be most useful to students and improve the impact these tasks had.
- When thought about carefully for the whole GCSE, this took a great deal of time.

As subject leader, I assigned distributed retrieval topics to each lesson in the course.

- We mixed tasks focused on consolidating the current topic with interleaved retrieval tasks from previous units.
- This was drawn up as one document to ensure even coverage of topics across the course.

As a team, we shared the design of retrieval tasks.

- We did some training around including some tasks that mirrored the retrieval processes which students undertook in exams.
- These were entirely focused on the identified core content.
- Answers were added to slides to make the delivery smoother and quicker.

We used every resource available to us.

- Significant amounts of meeting time were put into identifying core content and collaboratively planning tasks.
- Our ITE mentor, Emily Harrison, supported our trainee teacher colleagues to gain a great deal from exploring the core content of the GCSE, reflecting on the retrieval need and designing some tasks. We gained a few more retrieval practice tasks in return.

At the time of writing, we are yet to see the effect of this implementation across a full two-year course finished with a full set of exams, due to the disruption of the coronavirus pandemic. I am hopeful however that this structured and focused approach to retrieval practice, carefully tuned to the needs of history, will have a significant impact on the outcomes of our students.

Thank you to Hugh for sharing his experiences and insight. You can follow Hugh on Twitter @HughJRichards and learn more about Huntington Research School @HuntResearchSch.

James Maxwell is Headteacher at Carrickfergus Grammar School in Northern Ireland and is also the author of *Making Every MFL lesson count: Six Principles to Support Modern Foreign Language Teaching.* I have had the privilege to work with James and his enthusiastic team of teachers. As a headteacher, naturally James has oversight of teaching, learning, curriculum and professional development at his school. He shares the approach he has taken in terms of whole-school leadership with retrieval practice.

Whole-school leadership and retrieval practice

James Maxwell

Increasingly, direction in my school has been shaped by educational research. That journey started when we read Daniel Willingham's seminal book *Why Don't Students Like School?* It was a game-changer which led us onto other great educational literature such as Daisy Christodoulou's *Making Good Progress? The Future of Assessment for Learning* and Peps McCrea's *Memorable Teaching.* A staff training day in 2019 focused on some of this literature and the decision was taken to embed the following three maxims as the crux of our learning and teaching principles in our new School Development Plan:

- Subject-specific knowledge must precede domain-specific skill;

- Memory is the residue of thought; and

- Assessment is the bridge between learning and teaching.

At Carrickfergus Grammar School we are convinced that the one thing which underpins the aforementioned maxims is highly effective retrieval practice. We know that there is a difference between performance and real learning. Students may perform well on an end-of-unit test after the content has just been taught but may underperform significantly when assessed on the same content in an exam four months later. This may well be because the content has not embedded in long-term memory. If real learning involves a change in the 'mental map' in our long-term memory, then effective retrieval practice is most certainly a solid, steady and secure bridge between our teaching of content and that end goal. For us at Carrickfergus Grammar School, the development of effective retrieval practice strategies holds such importance that it is now our key, core CPD priority. Too often in schools, there is a danger that CPD can become a 'tick-box' exercise, particularly when schools are at the mercy of the whims of LEAs, curriculum or exam advisory bodies. I'm reminded of an anecdote I heard of a school where the principal stood up and said, 'We have done assessment for learning in our CPD, it's now concluded, and next year we move on to something else'.

When I say that effective retrieval practice is a key and core CPD priority at our school, I mean that it will remain our key and core priority – year after year – because the evidence regarding the impact of retrieval practice is so consistent and robust. This isn't an 'educational fad' like many other things schools are often 'coerced' into doing. Retrieval practice has an impact and makes a difference to our students' outcomes, and it can help give our students the edge in later life.

When I reflect on my journey as a teacher, like many others I think I always was aware sub-consciously of the importance of retrieval. In 2014 the Sutton Trust report, entitled 'What makes great teaching?', concluded that the (pedagogical) content knowledge of the teacher has one of the strongest impacts on student outcomes. I was not surprised that the report also concluded that 'pedagogical content knowledge' did not just include teachers' subject knowledge but also their ability to plan for and identify potential misconceptions on the part of students in their learning and respond accordingly. However, it was only upon reading Kate Jones' excellent book on retrieval practice when it was published in 2019 that I started to think explicitly about retrieval strategies and the hugely powerful role they have in affording teachers opportunities to identify misconceptions (just think as a very simple example about the feedback we receive when 30 children are holding up mini-whiteboard responses in front of us), and the vital role retrieval strategies can play in our responsive teaching. Kate's book was an eye-opener and as a result at Carrickfergus Grammar School we secured a copy of the book for each member of staff which we now affectionately refer to it as 'Kate's pink book'. And thus began our explicit journey at school with retrieval practice.

Step 1: The first question we asked was 'why retrieval?' As teachers, we instinctively know what works and what doesn't, and we incline towards 'common sense'. I would argue that (subconsciously at least) many teachers know that low stakes, formative quizzing and testing in lessons is impactful. Therefore, the rationale for retrieval is made easier in this regard. However, the section in Kate's 'pink book' about the rationale for retrieval and associated research was our starting point.

Step 2: The leadership team in school decided to allocate a staff development day purely and simply to allow staff to read research – from home, from Costa Coffee, from the top of a mountain, from wherever they wanted to be. We didn't care where they read, just as long as they read. To aid this process, we put together a folder of research and articles based on retrieval, as well as directing staff to Kate's book. This was light-touch. There was no big 'checking-up' by leadership afterwards as to what staff had read and what they had 'learned'. In my experience, just allowing staff to 'step back' from their very busy teaching schedules for a day and focus on research is enough of a gain. Although staff will not have time to read everything, they will take away from the experience little 'nuggets' of thinking, particularly about how it may translate into their own subject areas. That, too, is a sizeable gain.

Step 3: In school, I then asked two of my teachers who had already been 'ploughing a bit of a furrow' with retrieval in their own respective classrooms to prepare a presentation to staff about retrieval, focusing on the rationale and giving some initial thoughts about strategies which could be employed within classrooms. This was delivered in a 45-minute session during a follow-up training day. Having two practising teachers who were both internal to the school delivering this training heightened its validity and appeal which, I believe, was helped even more so by the high-quality of delivery. Interest in the presentation was such that the question and answer session afterwards lasted about 20 minutes with teachers sharing their own experiences and pondering further questions such as how to break the misconception that retrieval is reductive and focused solely on factual knowledge, but rather how it can be used to get pupils to think deeper, to think analytically, to apply knowledge.

Step 4: As a school leader, I believe that CPD is at its best when it is somewhat 'organic', i.e. when a general steer from the top is married by organic approaches being developed within subject departments. In an excellent blog post by Tom Sherrington (2020) he concluded that 'whole-school teaching and learning programmes need to combine general principles with strong ground-up implementation'. At Carrickfergus Grammar School, our general principle was the development of effective retrieval practice strategies within lessons, and step 4 involved departments in school deciding upon and trialling low stakes retrieval techniques within their lessons from the 'ground-up', based on a perception about what might work best for that subject. Examples are as follows:

Chemistry decided to trial Adam Boxer's retrieval roulette, placing ten questions on the board at the start of each lesson, most linked to the current topic, others from topics undertaken weeks or months ago. Physics were trialling knowledge organisers and developed their knowledge organisers for student self-quizzing, with questions on one side of the page and answers on the other, and with templates which included only questions and no answer. Students self-quizzed regularly both at home and in class. Maths trailed the use of mini-whiteboards in lessons for the purposes of retrieval linked to consolidating strong mental maths. Modern languages used techniques such as: A 'do-now' challenge, which requires students to retrieve vocabulary, conjugate from memory, find the odd-one-out and translate; a 'five-a-day' challenge in which students must conjugate, list (e.g. adjectives on a topic), spot the odd-one-out, correct a mistake and translate a sentence; and a 'Connect 4' theme in which students must translate four words in separate discs of the same colour. Other tasks included retrieval challenge grids whereby they get one point for retrieval of a word from the last lesson, two points for last week's lesson, three points for last month's lesson and four points for last year's lesson. History explored online approaches such as Quizlet Live and Quizizz.

Step 5: To develop our evidence-base framework further, the school designed and launched a CPD portal for staff, in which we brought together and collated useful online articles, some from researchers and authors, others from practising teachers writing practice in their classrooms. Linked to this, we subscribed to Oliver Caviglioli and Tom Sherrington's 'WalkThru' packages and made this an online resource for staff, including further guidance on retrieval.

Step 6: As we developed our explicit thinking and understanding of retrieval within the school, we realised that there were common questions we were grappling with between departments, such as how we ensure that retrieval is integral throughout our lessons and not just something which 'is done' for five to ten minutes at the start, and how we ensure that we are using it effectively to develop higher-order thinking, and how we construct our questions to deepen thinking. At this stage, we 'asked the expert'. We were delighted to be able to hold a one-hour Zoom session with Kate herself who understood that the school had at this stage moved far beyond the 'why retrieval' stage and that we were at the stage of 'honing' strategies. Consequently, her presentation to us focused on the misconceptions about retrieval, such as limiting it to one small part of the lesson and the mistakes which are often made in the construction of retrieval questions. It was an excellent session which inspired staff, and which has helped to develop and deepen our own understanding of retrieval in action.

If you were to come to visit Carrickfergus Grammar School now, I would be fairly confident that you would see retrieval in action just by talking a short walk around the school. If you were to ask any of our students, they would be able to tell you explicitly about retrieval in their respective classrooms, about how teachers adapt spacing and interleaving strategies, and how it impacts positively on their learning. Like teachers, students too have an in-built radar for 'what works' and our students know well that 'retrieval works'. They are seeing the outworkings of it in their test and exam results, but also on a day-to-day basis in their classroom answers.

For me, one of the biggest wins came in a recent school survey to parents, in which we asked them if their child had ever discussed retrieval with them at home, and how retrieval strategies were being implemented in classrooms. Over 75% of parents said that their child had indeed done so. For me as a school leader, that was the icing on the cake and a clear sign that retrieval is now at the heart of everything we are doing with learning and teaching at Carrickfergus Grammar School.

It was a pleasure and privilege for me to work with staff at Carrickfergus Grammar School. Thank you to James for sharing his leadership reflections and advice. You can follow James on Twitter @Ni_Principal.

Retrieval practice and SEND students

Often teachers wonder if retrieval practice really is the most appropriate strategy for *all* of the learners in their classroom, I initially pondered this question myself. It can be a worry that some students might not respond well to retrieval practice and, despite the low stakes nature, some may still find the act of quizzing stressful. In the past when I have been asked 'is retrieval practice a strategy for SEND[5] learners?' my immediate reaction has been absolutely! However, I think it was too hasty and whilst I do still advocate it as a teaching and learning strategy for all learners it is clear when it comes to SEND students that a lot of support and adaptation is required with recall.

One example of this could be students with ADHD. Students with ADHD are more likely to encounter academic difficulties, inside and outside of the classroom. ADHD students can struggle to keep up with the pace in a lesson and may also find the concept of remote learning working at home independently without teacher support very difficult.

Knouse, Rawson and Dunlosky (2020) published their study which concluded that 'Undergraduate students with ADHD may benefit

---

5   Special educational needs and disability.

from retrieval practice but may have difficulty using this strategy consistently'. After carrying out various testing to find out whether students with ADHD benefitted as much as non–ADHD students from self-regulated retrieval practice the results showed that 'recall and recognition were as high for students with ADHD as those without ADHD, regardless of whether students regulated their learning or were forced to achieve criterion. Among those who regulated their learning, students with and without ADHD used retrieval practice and feedback to a similar degree. Results support recommending retrieval practice to criterion for college students with and without ADHD.'

I have been searching academic research for more answers about SEND and retrieval practice but something I should do more of in terms of this field is speak to teachers, leaders and experts who can share their experiences and expertise. Jules Daulby specialises in supporting students with SEND and assisting teachers to better support their SEND learners too. Jules was able to share with me a lot of insight and guidance. Firstly, we need to remember students with dyslexia, ADHD and other learning difficulties will require much longer. This is something for us to be mindful of when we consider how many questions we ask and how much time we provide. Jules explained that a lot of SEND students will take longer and need more practice. She says that the simple answer is that many retrieval and interleaving strategies are great for children with SEND. But they may not retain it long term. This is why repeated retrieval with prompts, cues and scaffolding are so important. Jules added that, from experience, most can perform retrieval but they lose the information quicker. It helps if SEND students have information encoded through stories, rhymes, say it, hear it and see it with multi-sensory experiences and lots of visual prompts. Jules is an advocate for having high but realistic expectations with SEND students.

In the same vein as gender differences, it is clear that more research is required into the use of retrieval practice with students with learning difficulties but the current research and evidence should give us the confidence to persevere with this strategy with all the learners in our classroom. Support staff that spend time working with students with learning challenges should also be equipped with background knowledge and an understanding of retrieval practice and the benefits for learners.

Forgetting

There's been a lot of discussion about forgetting and retrieval but that discussion tends to focus on the implications of Ebbinghaus' forgetting curve. Despite the fact this experiment has been replicated many times, with similar findings, it was carried out in 1885! What does the latest research tell us about forgetting? Bjork and Bjork (2019) published research which found one of the peculiarities of human learning is that there can be certain conditions that produce forgetting and create opportunities to enhance our level of learning. They wrote: 'It is natural to think that learning consists of building up knowledge or skills in our memories and that forgetting is losing some of what was built up. The relationship between learning and forgetting, however, is not so simple and is, in some respects, quite the opposite.' This is an example of research challenging our long-held beliefs and practices, making us think differently and consider an alternative approach to teaching. The examples of conditions that induce forgetting but enhance learning that Bjork and Bjork are referring to include varying the learning environments and increasing the interval between study opportunities (this is achieved with spaced practice).

Varying the environmental contexts may seem unusual because we tend to design lessons so that they take place in the same location for each learning session: the classroom. We also instruct students to find a calm and quiet workspace and make that their go-to place for studying outside of the classroom. Realistically, we can't move students around the school to teach lessons in different locations, it might be possible but it will be a logistical nightmare. In terms of studying outside of school, it can be easier for students to use different locations from a room in their home to a library. Bjork and Bjork summarise in their study: 'When something is initially studied in a particular environmental location and then tested later, there tends to be a "context effect" – namely, that the material studied is more recallable when tested in the same context where it was studied than when tested in a different environmental context. If, however, rather than being tested, the material is restudied, either in the same location or a different location, and recall is then tested in some new setting at a later time, the pattern is very different. Having restudied the material in a different location where more of it will have been forgotten at the time of this restudy, rather than the original location where more of it will still be accessible at the time of this restudy, actually enhances later recall of that material'. This is very interesting and something we can share with students and parents, encouraging them to vary the environment where they study.

In terms of increasing the interval between study opportunities with spaced practice, this has always gone hand in hand with retrieval practice for me. Spaced retrieval practice is simply the best form of retrieval practice. It can be difficult to implement at first and students aren't always receptive to it, preferring cramming and blocking instead of interleaving. Bjork and Bjork explain further: 'Related to the benefits of spacing, interleaving the study or practice of the separate components of to-be-learned material or skills can induce forgetting, but enhance learning.' It appears to something of a double-edged sword and a bizarre concept; promoting forgetting to enhance learning.

Bjork and Bjork have carried out numerous studies on the impact of spaced retrieval practice and interleaving. In recent years the benefits of interleaving have also been demonstrated with verbal and conceptual tasks. Bjork and Bjork add: 'Again, these findings suggest that standard practices of teaching are often not optimal. Teachers are susceptible to thinking that blocking instruction by problem type or domain helps students, whereas interleaving such instruction might cause confusion.' The advice is clear, the implementation isn't as clear. As well as interrupting the forgetting curve we need to be planning and ensuring there are opportunities for forgetting to occur to support long-term learning.

Another area of research in terms of retrieval practice and forgetting to be aware of is retrieval-induced forgetting. This is where the recall of specific information can impact the forgetting of other information. There has been a lot of discussion of this in academia since the '90s and research continues in this area, but it is not as widely discussed in education. Bjork, Bjork and Storm (2008) found that items that suffer from retrieval-induced forgetting benefit more from relearning than control items. They demonstrated that retrieval success is not a necessary condition for retrieval-induced forgetting to occur.

To understand the concept of retrieval-induced forgetting Bjork and Bjork (2012) provides this example of a study that was carried out: 'When participants are prompted to retrieve with cues that have no possible answer (FRUIT: WO_____, rather than the standard, FRUIT: OR_____), access to competing items (BANANA) is impaired, as demonstrated on a final recall test. Furthermore, we are currently exploring the impact of variations of the type of cue support provided for retrieval attempts (FRUIT: OR_____; FISH: _____ORE; WEAPONS: DAGG_____).

Our efforts in this domain currently rest on testing various assumptions of theoretical accounts of retrieval–induced forgetting.' What impact does this have on education? It is a retrieval practice paradigm, practising recall of specific information can potentially impair non-tested material. However, to combat this we simply need to think carefully about what we want and need our students to be able to recall from long-term memory. Focus on that and accept that some information will be forgotten but if it is important then have students regularly retrieve it.

Retrieval practice and higher-order thinking

Tomas Needham is an English teacher and director of research at Trinity School, Lewisham. I have thoroughly enjoyed reading blogs Tomas has written. He represents the modern teacher blogger; engaging with evidence, implementing research into his classroom practice and then reflecting and sharing through writing. Tomas writes about retrieval practice going beyond factual recall and has drawn on the research of a leading academic in this field, Professor Pooja K. Agarwal in addition to his own classroom experiences.

Should practice tests look like final tests?

Tom Needham

For many subjects at school, the final performance is often extended writing where students are expected to combine multiple individual components within a coherent essay. Top marks are awarded to those students who can retrieve and apply an impressive range of knowledge and skills. So how can a quiz help with this complex performance? Can retrieval practice help students write better essays? If so, are some forms of retrieval better suited to this goal than others? How can we decide which approach to use and when to use it? Retrieval practice can range from closed, factual questions to higher-order questions to open-ended free recall tasks where students are asked to write down everything that they know on a particular topic. Here are some examples:

- Closed, factual question: What does 'paranoid' mean?

- Higher-order question: Why is Macbeth paranoid in Act 3?

■ Free recall question: Write down everything you know about Macbeth's paranoia.

Agarwal (2019) explored the efficacy of different forms of retrieval practice. She concluded that closed unconnected 'fact' quizzing will not help students perform well in higher-order tasks. Agarwal also concluded that for higher-order tasks like essays, the best approach would be to ask higher-order questions in retrieval practice. So does that mean that the closed, factual question is pointless? If it is the only question style that is asked, then the answer is probably yes. However, if the question forms the start of a series of questions, each one asking students to think a little broader and wider about the topic, then it may be part of a useful, scaffolded retrieval task. For retrieval practice to be effective, students need to be able to successfully retrieve the information and a series of questions that begin with a closed factual question can be an efficient way to get students to make connections whilst also ensuring that retrieval success is consistently high. After each question in the chain, the teacher can give feedback and tell them the answer, helping those students who are struggling. This is what a chain of scaffolded retrieval questions might look like:

1. What does 'paranoid' mean?

2. What is the noun for 'paranoid'?

3. Complete the quotation: 'Oh full of sc....... is my mind.'

4. What are the connotations of 'scorpions'?

5. Complete the quotation: 'Sleep in the infl....... of these t....... dreams.'

6. After killing Duncan, Macbeth exclaims: 'Macbeth does m....... sl.......'

7. Explore Macbeth's paranoia.

The final question is a higher-order question: it is far more similar to the kind of questions that they would get in an examination and will require them to analyse and synthesise information. So why not skip straight to the final question? Why ask the questions beforehand? If students were merely asked the higher-order question, it is likely they would not be able to retrieve the required information, or they may not organise and connect it in an optimal fashion. Students often need help with making links between components and bits of knowledge and chains of lower-order questions can help facilitate this. An additional benefit of these chains of questions is that the teacher can give precise corrective feedback after each one. This is much harder to do in response to higher-order tasks where errors may be widespread. These chains of questions are well suited to the early stages of a unit where one of the most important jobs that the teacher can do is building the knowledge base of the students that they are teaching. If students are to maintain consistently high success levels – something crucial for motivation – then splitting higher-order performances into chains of purpose, connected, questioning can be really helpful. Initial retrieval tasks should involve closed questions to firm components. They should be followed by connecting questions to help students make links between individual items and the final questions should be higher-order so that students can then apply the connected components in extended answers. It's a bit like building. Each brick of knowledge needs to be firmed and solid before being connected to others in increasingly larger constructions: sentences, paragraphs and then whole essays.

Thanks to Tomas for sharing his classroom practice and reflections. You can follow Tomas on Twitter @Tom_Needham_ and visit his teaching and learning blog tomneedhamteach. wordpress.com.

Multiple-choice questions

Each multiple-choice should contain a stem (the question), the correct answer and distractors (other plausible options). Multiple-choice questioning (MCQ) has become a popular form of low stakes quizzing. Students enjoy this style of quiz and there is a range of benefits in terms of using this quizzing technique in the classroom, however, as the following table shows, this is not a perfect classroom strategy but no classroom strategy is. The following are some pros and cons to consider and be mindful of when using multiple choice questioning.

Pros	Cons
MCQs can be used for formative and summative assessment but lend themselves well to low stakes quizzing.	If MCQs are used for end of unit tests or any form of high stakes assessment it can be difficult for them to be viewed as a low stakes retrieval task by learners. Some students will make the distinction but using different tools can support this, e.g. Quizzizz for low stakes quizzing and Google Forms for assessment for example.
MCQs can provide retrieval support for younger students and students with learning difficulties making retrieval practice more accessible and the challenge desirable. They can be differentiated through question design.	If questions are not designed well they will not require effortful retrieval – it will more likely involve low-level recognition or power of elimination.
MCQs can lead to opportunities for retrieval success, this can increase motivation and confidence for learners.	There is potential for guesswork. It can be very difficult for teachers to know if students recalled correct information or simply guessed (although they are likely to be more reliable than simple true/false) and there are ways to tackle this, which I will discuss.
MCQs can be a quizzing activity that can be flexible in terms of time spent in a lesson. MCQs can be delivered relatively quickly, not dominating lesson time so more time can be used for feedback and discussion.	Some online quizzing tools use timers and award points to students depending on the speed of their answers. This encourages students to rush, not read questions carefully and make errors.
MCQs, when designed carefully, can address potential misconceptions or misunderstandings that may have developed in previous lessons, this is useful for the teacher to be aware of.	Students do not always check and reflect on their answers. Preferring to view scores rather than identify and address the gaps in their knowledge.
They are graded and scored objectively – answers are either right or wrong, no need for moderation or review.	There is no flexibility in terms of credit – either incorrect or correct even if the students have some knowledge linked to the question that will be not awarded or recognised.

MCQs quizzing can be a workload friendly option for teachers, especially with technology. MCQs can provide instant feedback to students digitally and/or can be self or peer-assessed. Questions and quizzes can be reused at a later date, spaced retrieval and with different classes covering the same content.	Creating carefully designed questions and plausible options can be time-consuming. A good way to address this is to view other teachers quizzes and take/teleport/ adapt questions or work together within a department or phase.
MCQs work well across all ranges and subjects. There is a vast range of excellent online MCQ quizzing tools such as Google Forms, Microsoft Forms, Quizizz, Quizlet, Kahoot and more. This style of quiz can also be carried out without technology too.	As a retrieval strategy it has limitations. We must provide opportunities for free recall too, teachers should not rely solely on MCQs for retrieval practice. Other strategies should be used in addition to MCQs.
MCQs can be versatile in terms of the content and type of questions asked which can range from factual recall to higher-order thinking if the questions are carefully crafted.	Designing carefully constructed MCQs can be difficult, not just in terms of writing the questions but trying to create plausible options (distractors). Not always easy to do.

Andrew Butler (2018) wrote: 'Multiple-choice tests are arguably the most popular type of assessment in education, and much research has been dedicated to determining best practices for using them to measure learning. The act of taking a test also causes learning, and numerous studies have investigated how best to use multiple-choice tests to improve long-term retention and produce deeper understanding.' In this article, Butler investigated and explored whether the best practices used for assessment also align with the best practices for learning, as retrieval practice is a learning tool rather than an assessment tool. I found this research paper to be very interesting and certainly has immediate implications for teachers when it comes to designing MCQs as a retrieval task.

MCQ top tips

Based on the recommendations from Butler, other teachers and my own classroom experiences, I have included some top tips to consider when it comes to creating and using MCQs:

- Avoid using complex question styles or answer formats. Complexity with retrieval practice can cause confusion, misunderstanding and students can resort to guesswork instead of recall. Keep it super simple in terms of the phrasing and layout of the question so that MCQs are genuinely providing opportunities for retrieval practice.

- Consider the language and terminology used, linking to the previous point. Unless the question is focusing on vocabulary it is advisable to use tier two vocabulary rather than tier three so all students can understand what the question is asking. I teach in an international setting and often words can have different meanings depending on a person's background,[6] this is something to consider with our explanations as well as question designing and phrasing.

- Design questions that require precise recall. Ensure that questions focus on specific aspects of knowledge, concepts, content or thought processes that you want to assess. Question design is discussed more thoroughly in the next chapter but it should align with the curriculum rather than be generalised trivia, sometimes trivia questions are included ('let's stick an interesting or random question in!') but are not necessary.

- Avoid using 'none of the above'. The review by Butler explains that the issue with this approach is that if the correct option is 'none of the above' then we have simply wasted time and exposed students to a range of incorrect answers. We want students to be retrieving and selecting the correct answer and this type of question takes that opportunity away from them. A wasted retrieval opportunity. I never use 'none of the above' but I have previously created questions where the correct answer was 'all of the above', which links to my next point.

- Avoid using 'all of the above' as the correct answer. I thought this strategy would check if students were reading the questions and answers carefully but then this might appear as though we are trying to trick the students. There is also an issue if a student selects an answer other than 'all of the above', this will be classed as incorrect when in fact it is a correct answer in addition to the other options, it's just not the exact answer you were looking for. Linking back to the first suggestion, we are trying to avoid confusion.

- Use three plausible response options. I have seen so many multiple choice quizzes online where the issue and problem isn't the question itself but the options provided. At times the options can be so absurd and plainly incorrect that retrieval isn't even required. Anybody could simply answer based on the power of elimination or common sense. Busch (2018) advises 'the topic will have a bearing on the optimal

---

6   For example, I once asked if anyone in the class had a rubber. My students from the USA were horrified but I clearly explained I was referring to an eraser!

number to offer, but three potential answers usually provides enough difficulty whilst also being time efficient.'

- Avoid opinion–based questions or where there is the possibility of debate, MCQs are not the right platform for it.

- Include the option 'I don't know yet'. This links in with the growth mindset approach of not knowing *yet*. It also encourages students to be honest and avoid guessing. This will be more insightful for the teacher in comparison to trying to figure out if a student was able to recall the correct answer, had an educated guess or simply a lucky guess!

- Create MCQs that do provide a degree of challenge because the style of the question itself already offers support by presenting the student with the correct answer, albeit alongside incorrect options. This is something that is continually referred to in this book and has become well-known as 'desirable difficulties', based on the work of Bjork and Bjork. The goldilocks principles of getting it 'just right' applies; if it is too easy or too hard then little will be learned. Busch (2018) quotes Butler who states that 'the ideal difficulty level is a bit higher than the midpoint between chance and perfect performance'.

- Aim to keep the stem a question, instead of 'which of the following is' or 'which of the following is not'. Learners may miss the point of the stem.

- Keep the level of depth for each distractor option the same, e.g. all one word or all extended sentences. More depth for the correct answer can be a giveaway.

- Put options/distractors in a vertical format all with the same lower or upper case, again just for clarity. Shuffle up the answers so the correct answer isn't always B or C, online quizzing tools do this automatically. Keep MCQs crystal clear in terms of layout and design.

- Ensure feedback is provided. This is advice I am continually encountering and based on my reflections, I realised feedback and reflection time is something I have skimmed previously or not dedicated enough time to.

Blake Harvard is an American educator and blogger, specialising in cognitive psychology and bridging the gap between academic research and the classroom. Harvard has carried out extensive work on how MCQs can be used effectively and his writings have helped me significantly with my own classroom practice. In this case study, Harvard explains how he encourages his students to think more deeply and carefully about their responses with MCQs, as well as using this as an opportunity to include dual coding and promote reflection. This strategy will take longer but with MCQs a 'less is more approach' can be more effective.

Maximising the effectiveness of multiple-choice questions
Blake Harvard

A quick activity that is easily adaptable for most class settings is included on the next page. It maximises the effectiveness of multiple-choice questions and is a wonderful way for students and teachers to assess student learning. I really like this activity, because unlike most involving multiple-choice questions, this template makes use of all answer choices and requires students to effortfully work with all of the material. Another reason I like this activity is its ability to cover a lot of material in a few questions. If you have ten questions with five answer choices, the students could feasibly interact with 50 different snippets of material. As you can see, the student has to interact with the question stems in various ways:

- With the correct answer, the student must either provide a memory aid they used to help them choose this answer *or* provide a sketch that illustrates the term or concept covered.

- With the incorrect answers, students must:

  - Use the 'trickiest' incorrect answer to describe why this answer is most likely to trip up students and potentially lead students in choosing this answer.

  - Rewrite the question to make this incorrect answer the correct answer.

  - Give an example relating this answer to the student's life.

  - Link this answer to information from a previous lesson/unit or learned from another class.

1. Question here A. B. C. D. E.	_____ ← Correct answer here Provide a memory aid used OR an illustration of the answer.
_____ ← Incorrect answer here Why might someone incorrectly choose this answer? What is tricky or confusing about this answer that makes it the 'best' wrong answer?	
_____ ← Incorrect answer here Rewrite the question to make this incorrect answer the correct answer.	
_____ ← Incorrect answer here Give an example relating this answer to your life.	
_____ ← Incorrect answer here Link this answer to information from a previous lesson/unit or class. How does this information relate to prior material?	

Harvard poses these questions to teachers:

- How can you use this in your class?

- How could you modify the template for use as a study guide, for homework, or as a quiz grade in class?

- What other ideas do you have to help students interact with the answers?

Thank you to Blake for sharing this excellent idea. You can follow him on Twitter @effortfuleduktr and visit his superb teaching and learning blog theeffortfuleducator.com.

Another strategy can be to use a confidence rating, students rank their levels of confidence either in numerical order or selecting an emoji before they know whether the answer is correct or not. This can be useful for the teacher to gain insight into their level of confidence about their ability to recall precise information as well as useful for the student when considering which answer they are selecting.

I was surprised by how much information is available about MCQs from academic research to classroom teachers sharing their advice and reflections. Further research is also being carried out into the effectiveness and impact of MCQs on learning. Taking this discussion of MCQs even further, in the next chapter I explore some common mistakes made when it comes to MCQs and offer advice as to how we can avoid these. In chapter 3 I recommend a range of brilliant online quizzing tools that can be used for MCQs.

Retrieval practice and CPD

Reading educational books has become one of my favourite forms of professional learning. There are so many books available for teachers that we are spoilt for choice! On the other hand, trying to keep up with the pace of books being published can be difficult and the sheer volume is intimidating at times. Of course, we simply cannot and should not read all the educational books out there. It's OK to be selective and pick books that link with our specific areas for professional development. In recent years I have read a considerable amount of books linked to cognitive psychology. I am very interested in this field as a classroom teacher and middle leader and this has supported my research and writing as an author. I am aware of the fact there has been imbalance so I have made a conscious effort to read books that will further enhance and deepen my subject knowledge in addition to books that will help me develop as a leader. Professional learning does need to be well-rounded but at the same time should be focused on specific areas. Professional learning should be linked to daily classroom practice and students outcomes. Retrieval practice is such an effective classroom strategy, therefore schools must be factoring in learning about retrieval practice with ongoing professional development.

Dylan Wiliam regularly discusses and writes about the importance of continual professional development and learning for teachers.

Wiliam (2018) has stated 'the quality of teaching is arguably the single most important thing that teachers and school leaders can focus on to make a difference in children's learning. The difference between really good teaching and less effective teaching makes more difference to learning than any other factor within a school'. Professional learning matters. It is a very significant factor in determining students' learning and outcomes. Whilst there can and should be targets and goals, professional learning is also never-ending and should be consistent throughout our careers regardless of experience or role.

Kane, Rockoff and Staiger (2008) have suggested teachers typically plateau after three to five years and highlight there is little evidence that improvement continues after three years. Ladd (2008) found on average, teachers with twenty years of experience are not much more effective than those with five years. These findings are not very hopeful or positive but should not discredit or dismiss teacher experience. We know CPD matters but we also all know that not all CPD is helpful or effective. Professional learning is complex and it's true that when it comes to whole-school professional learning, one size does not fit all. Taking retrieval practice as an example; teachers across a school or even a department can have different levels of prior knowledge and understanding, different levels of confidence using this strategy and it can be difficult to assess the consistency in terms of implementing this technique into classroom practice.

Where are we going wrong with professional learning and with the context of retrieval practice too? The first error occurs if schools and leaders do not prioritise professional learning and are not providing opportunities for staff to learn, implement, embed and reflect. It's no good sharing a PowerPoint or infographic with what appears to be the latest buzzword on the scene. It has to be much more than that. If retrieval practice has been presented to staff in the same manner other strategies have – those that haven't been properly implemented and embedded – then it's no wonder staff will view retrieval as another fad. Retrieval practice is here to stay, both in the classroom and with professional learning. Previously in schools, there have been too many new initiatives forced upon staff. Instead of focusing on something new each term or academic year the focus can shift to doing the same but better.

Retrieval practice can be vulnerable to mutation and poor implementation. Quality assurance will be key when it comes to effectively using retrieval practice in the classroom. Quality assurance is important both in terms of internal and external professional development. Is there a member of staff that has taken an interest in retrieval practice, demonstrated that they have read widely and carefully considered how they use this in their classroom? This could be a good opportunity for sharing best practice at a departmental or whole-school level. There are plenty of books (I appreciate the irony here) and/or useful research papers, articles or blogs that can be distributed to staff to learn more about retrieval practice (a link to further online resources about retrieval practice can be found at the back of this book).

2020 was the year for online webinars and there are presentations easily and freely accessible online for teachers to view about retrieval practice, in addition to a range of high-quality professional learning courses (varying from free to fee). The key is that all forms of professional learning linked to retrieval practice directly links back to classroom practice. To do this teachers will need to engage with the theory and evidence but also put this theory into action in the classroom then regularly evaluate the impact.

I am incredibly lucky to work at the school I do and the context of the school (a not-for-profit leading British curriculum school in Abu Dhabi) does mean that the school can follow through with their promise to passionately and financially support all staff with their professional learning needs. As a school, cognitive science is one of our four teaching and learning areas of focus alongside questioning, literacy and feedback. The priorities have been the same for three years because long-lasting and effective change takes time. We have opportunities to discuss, share and reflect on these teaching and learning priorities collectively as a staff, collaborate as middle leaders in addition to an in-depth focus within departments. This was a crucial factor in my decision to join the school. Schools should be asking teachers 'what do you do for your own professional development and learning?' Teachers should be asking schools 'how will you support my professional development and learning?'

The infographic that follows is one I created[7] to show the different ways staff can learn and develop, in a broader sense or specifically to retrieval practice.

---

7   I know, I know! Another jigsaw. But I do like the jigsaw concept for explaining how factors are explicitly linked and connected!

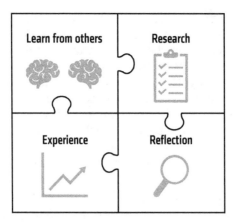

The first piece of the puzzle, learning from others, is something we can and should be doing daily, but it is often a strategy that isn't fully utilised. Learning from others can be informal, ranging from conversations to learning walks or internal presentations. We can learn from other teachers and leaders externally through engaging with blogs, books, subject associations and leading experts. The second piece of the puzzle, engaging with research, is vital if a school truly wishes to become evidence-informed. There are challenges in accessing academic research from paywalls to finding the time to do so but research is now more accessible than ever before. Classroom experiences can be shared with others through discussions, meetings and writing. All linking explicitly to the final piece of the puzzle – reflection. How often do you reflect on your classroom practice? How do you do this? Do you reflect on your own? Do you record your reflections? Do you discuss and reflect with your line manager? Do you reflect collectively as a department or a whole-school body? As a leader, how do you support your team with their reflections? A lot of questions there for you to ponder and reflect on.

Closing the gap between research and practice

Thanks to excellent websites such as **retrievalpractice.org, innerdrive. com** and **thelearningscientists.org** academic research on the science of learning is now much more accessible for teachers, students and parents. Events such as researchEd have significantly helped connect academic researchers and classroom teachers around the world. These are fantastic events where presentations can be delivered by teachers, leaders at all levels and academics. The 2020 researchEd home presentations can be viewed on YouTube and features many superb sessions from academics and educators, many of whom are referenced in this book. Recent years have seen the teaching profession ditch a lot of nonsense and neuromyths in favour of taking a sensible and evidence-informed approach to teaching and learning. Research has, and continues to, invigorate the teaching profession.

This book contains a range of case studies from school teachers and leaders but I realised that for years I have been quoting academic research without actually engaging with any academic researchers and cognitive scientists, as I have done with educators. In an attempt to further close the gap between schools and academia, I decided to reach out to a group of renowned cognitive scientists and researchers to ask them to feature in this book. Much like teachers who are working hard to embrace academic research, many academics and cognitive scientists are passionately sharing the findings from research that has classroom implications and are reaching out to the teaching community through books, blogs, podcasts and presentations in addition to their published research. Thanks to the power of social media, email and Zoom I was able to have some truly fascinating conversations with leading experts in their fields. Both academics and educators grasp that retrieval practice is a powerful learning strategy but moving that conversation forward I posed the question, **'What is it you think teachers should or need to know about retrieval practice?'**

I do appreciate this can appear as a very complex question and to summarise an answer can be considered challenging (especially not knowing the context of what teachers already know or do not know about retrieval practice) but the responses I received were incredibly insightful. This question has essentially been the driving force behind my two books on retrieval practice: what is it we need to know as educators about retrieval practice to enhance our teaching and positively impact our students' learning?

Expert advice

I would like to thank all those who contributed to this book and took the time to discuss retrieval practice with me. It is a privilege to include their knowledge and advice. The responses about retrieval practice vary in terms of focus, including the generation effect, spaced practice, transfer of learning, motivation and more. The comments that follow are not quotes taken from a research paper but are direct responses in the hope that their knowledge and advice can support teachers and leaders in schools around the world implementing, embedding and reflecting on their use of retrieval practice.

Professor Henry L. Roediger III

If you have engaged with research relating to retrieval practice, you have likely come across Professor Roediger's work or his classic book *Make It Stick: The Science of Successful Learning*. Professor Roediger did comment that my question is certainly very complex and I agree! Here are his wonderful words of wisdom for teachers.

Teachers should know that retrieval practice works in helping students consolidate memories. A few tips on using it are:

1. Students should practice retrieval after some forgetting has occurred (that is, not immediately after studying) so it is effortful.

2. Correct answer feedback should always be given.

3. Spaced retrieval practice over long intervals should be given for critical concepts.

Professor Robert Bjork

Professor Robert Bjork is a Distinguished Research Professor in the Department of Psychology at UCLA and is very well known and internationally established in education, often described as the world's leading expert in memory. Working alongside his wife Elizabeth, the Bjorks have identified what perhaps should have been obvious to us all in education; the distinction between learning and performance. They also introduced the concept of 'desirable difficulties' in 'Making Things Hard on Yourself, But in a Good Way: Creating Desirable Difficulties to Enhance Learning', which has been regarded as a seminal paper in education. Based on his research and experiences, Professor Bjork offered the following suggestions to teachers.

My advice to teachers would be:

1. that whatever answer or procedure a teacher can get a student to generate will be far better recalled at a later time than any answer provided or illustrated to the student.

2. that the more involved or difficult the act of retrieval – provided it succeeds – the larger the benefits in terms of later recall.

3. that students can, and usually will, come to any new learning situation with differing degrees of prior relevant knowledge, so one very important skill for teachers to possess is asking questions in ways that are tuned to what prior knowledge a given student possesses. Often that will take the form of providing more cues to students who possess a less rich background in a given domain.

4. that even a failed effort to retrieve an answer or procedure can enhance subsequent learning when that answer or procedure is presented, but it is important for motivational and other reasons to have students succeed – though one skill of truly gifted teachers is encouraging a climate in which trying and making errors is encouraged.

Professor Elizabeth Bjork

Professor Elizabeth Bjork is a professor of psychology and Senior Vice-Chair in the psychology department at UCLA where she has also chaired UCLA's Academic Senate and received the Distinguished Teaching Award. Her main area of research has been the study of human memory and has published research alongside her husband Professor Robert Bjork.

She explained how she can find it discouraging speaking to teachers, trainers and instructors when few of them know about the research findings (referring to the work of Bjork and Bjork and others) that have strong implications for how students should study to enhance their learning. Professor Bjork also thanked me for trying to incorporate their work into my classroom teaching. I am sure you will agree that the following advice from Professor Bjork reads like liquid gold!

First, as you have probably observed, even the most motivated students – left to their own devices – will typically end up employing study strategies that involve the least amount of difficulty while seeming to produce rapid learning. One of the reasons that reading the same chapter over and over again is frequently reported by students as their most frequent and most preferred way to study. During that second reading, they experience a feeling of fluency and familiarity that indicates to them that they are mastering the material when, in fact, those feelings are typically arising owing to short-term priming effects and are not indicative of any long-term learning and deep understanding of the material. Thus, as teachers, we have to structure their study strategies in ways that force them to involve various sorts of 'desirable difficulties' so that they will be engaging in productive learning processes, such as spaced retrieval practice. One particularly productive procedure seems to be what has been referred to as 'expanding retrieval practice'. In this procedure, students are asked to retrieve the information that they are trying to encode and remember after intervals that begin fairly short (so that their retrieval will frequently be successful) but then over successive retrieval attempts the length of time since the previous one grows gradually longer. That is, as the instructor, you want to steadily increase the difficulty of successive retrievals while trying to find a level of difficulty that will allow some degree of success. One procedure that we have for years wanted to try, but have not yet had the opportunity to do so, is to try inserting questions into the reading of, say, a chapter or text passage, at increasing intervals of time as a possible way this might be accomplished.

Second, whatever you can do as an instructor to change students' attitudes about encountering difficulty in their studying from something negative to something positive would be a good thing. Students tend to interpret having difficulty with mastering a subject matter as meaning that it is just too hard for them to learn and leads to such thoughts as 'I'm just not smart enough to understand this subject; math/science is just not for me, and so forth.' If you can get them, instead, to start thinking of error not as indicating failure and an inability to learn the material but just as providing information about what they still need to learn, thus, errors are presenting them with opportunities to enhance their learning, we feel that would be a tremendous breakthrough for making their studying practices more effective and a step in leading them to a lifetime of productive learning. One way that might help with changing students' attitudes about errors is to give them pre-tests about some to-be-learned information (perhaps a text passage of some kind) before they are allowed to study it. They will make a lot of errors, but they will not look upon such errors as failures as they were not expected to have already learned that material, but just having attempted to ask such questions seems to then enhance their learning of the information to follow.

Third – although this is related to the second point – is that if you can convince students attempting to learn about some subject – even one about which they say they have no interest in learning – they will often then find themselves interested in that subject matter. I'm sure you have heard students say, 'Well if I was just interested in this stuff, I could learn it.' In fact, interest and learning go both ways. We can become very interested in something as a consequence of learning about it.[8]

Professor Pooja K. Agarwal

Pooja K. Agarwal is a cognitive scientist who has been conducting research on retrieval practice and how students learn since 2005. She is the co-author of the popular book *Powerful Teaching: Unleash the Science of Learning* and also the founder and creator of the website retrievalpractice.org This is a great site with guides, resources and blogs connected to the science of learning. I have been fortunate to be in contact with Professor Agarwal over recent years and she has been a great source of support, information and inspiration.

Professor Agarwal explains, with her winning combination of expertise and enthusiasm, how transfer is robust with retrieval practice. This is essential for all teachers to be aware of as transfer is the ultimate goal of long-term learning.

One reason I am so passionate about applying and implementing retrieval practice exercises in our classrooms is that there is so much research demonstrating that it truly does improve long-term learning for students of all ages, regardless of ability or content area. Retrieval practice is such a flexible strategy that it's effective for all learners. Transfer of learning, or simply 'transfer', is the application of learned concepts or information in new situations, from where learning originally took place. As educators, the fundamental goal of our instruction is that student learning inside our classroom will be applicable outside of our classroom, beyond a specific lesson, practice problem or diploma.

---

8   During the writing process of this book, the most enjoyable aspect has been the contact and exchanges between myself and the Bjorks. In addition to being accomplished, they are also very generous with their time, advice and support. In terms of heroes and role models, the Bjorks are mine!

By harnessing the science of learning we can use evidence-based strategies, such as retrieval practice, to foster students' transfer and application of knowledge to new situations.

If a student applies their learning in a new situation, then we can conclude that successful transfer has occurred. A critical factor in terms of transfer is that learners do not simply recall information; they have to use existing knowledge in new and different ways. Transfer is more than ordinary learning or remembering of an isolated topic or concept. Beyond ordinary learning, certain forms of retrieval practice are also quite effective at fostering transfer. These methods typically involve retrieving information more extensively and deeply than standard practice questions and exercises. This increased effort and broader engagement with the material can boost learning, understanding and transfer. Have students retrieve as much information as possible in meaningful and varied ways. Effective strategies include using broad retrieval exercises, constructing explanations and including a variety of questions. Have students retrieve not just one or two details from a lesson, but as much as they can possibly remember or everything they know about a specific topic because asking students to retrieve broadly encourages them to think about multiple aspects of the material to be learned and can result in improved transfer performance.

Paul A. Kirschner

Paul A. Kirschner is an acclaimed academic and author. His seminal paper with John Sweller and Richard E. Clark (2006), where learning was described as a change in long-term memory has been extensively quoted and has had a significant impact on education and how we view teaching and learning.

Kirschner is very well known in the online teaching community, he is active on Twitter (you can find him tweeting as @P_A_Kirschner) and a regular speaker at researchEd events. I felt incredibly lucky to be able to talk to him. Kirschner stated my question is not as complex as it seems but, in his opinion, quite easy to answer! The following is a summary of our conversation via Zoom.

Quite simply, students will not take our word for it, they need to experience the positive effects of retrieval practice for themselves. Kirschner further added that teachers need to teach retrieval practice explicitly and model exactly how it should be carried out, then teachers should practice regularly with learners and we should not assume that students will carry it out independently until they see 'what's in it for them'. Kirschner stressed that for students to use and embrace retrieval practice they need to be convinced it works and that can be achieved once they have experienced the positive effects. Students will be asking what's in it for me? How will I benefit from it? They will assume that retrieval practice will involve extra work for them and that it will not deliver results, but it does!

Kirschner explained how we can carry out natural experiments in the classroom, across a period of time with spaced retrieval with our classes. This will show students that retrieval practice does not cost extra effort, can lead to a better grade and reduce some of their test anxiety. Hearing and understanding at an intellectual level that retrieval practice works simply is not enough. Intellectually this strategy sounds good but they have to fully grasp and realise what they can achieve by using retrieval practice. This also applies to other evidence-informed approaches such as interleaving and spaced practice. Students have to experience that it works. 'Never forget that a student, just like the rest of us, is a homo economicus.'

Dr Jonathan G. Tullis

Dr Jonathan G. Tullis is Assistant Professor of Educational Psychology, Director of the Cognition And Memory in Education and Learning Lab, University of Arizona, and has had several peer reviews published. After reading and reflecting on his research, I contacted him to tell him about my interest in retrieval practice and ask for his insight. Professor Tullis had a simple yet important message that he felt was important to share with teachers.

Retrieval practice may seem ineffective, inefficient, or even painful, but practising retrieval brings an array of significant long-term learning benefits for students. Students and teachers rarely recognise the benefits of retrieval practice (because the benefits are non-intuitive), so they need to be explicitly taught about the benefits before they fully take advantage of retrieval practice to boost their learning.[9]

---

9   In the next chapter, I explore how we can explicitly explain the benefits of retrieval practice to everyone involved in the teaching and learning process including teachers, students and parents.

Dr Carolina Kuepper-Tetzel

Dr Carolina Kuepper-Tetzel is a lecturer in psychology at the University of Glasgow. She is an expert in applying findings from cognitive science to education and an enthusiastic science communicator.

Her expertise focuses on learning and memory phenomena that allow implementation in educational settings to offer teachers and students a wide range of strategies that promote long-term retention. Carolina is convinced that psychological research should serve the public and, to that end, engages heavily in scholarly outreach. You can follow her work via Twitter @pimpmymemory.

Retrieval from memory, whilst a powerful learning strategy, is a process that could be perceived as challenging for students. Of course, that's exactly one reason why retrieval practice is successful: We want students to engage in that effortful, successful process of retrieving previously-studied material from memory. However, as teachers, we need to make sure that all students have a chance to benefit from that strategy, i.e. that all students engage in the effortful but successful retrieval of the material. There are scenarios in the classroom that may undermine this goal. For example, asking questions and having students volunteer answers. You might find that you get quick responses from the same students over and over. This means that some students in the room may be missing out on the opportunity to practice retrieval. For that reason, I think the following two tips could help to make retrieval practice more inclusive:

1. In class, ask students to write down their answers individually. You can do this as a brief brain dumping exercise or have an online form ready with short-answer or multiple-choice questions. The advantage of the online form is that you can show students the summary of the responses of the entire class and discuss answers and correct misconceptions right away. I personally prefer that to brain dumping.

2. Post online forms with questions sometime after the class has happened. I like to do this because it first uses spaced practice which is another important learning strategy, but it also gives students thinking space. Coming up with a fleshed-out answer to a question in class can be perceived as stress-inducing. Instead, for more complex material, giving students

time to retrieve answers and produce a rich answer can be helpful. I have seen students come up with fantastic answers to more complex questions and make connections between ideas in this scenario.

To conclude, retrieval practice is great, but try to think of ways to make it as inclusive as possible for all students in your class.

Professor John Hattie

Professor John Hattie is Laureate Professor and Director at the Melbourne Graduate School of Education and Chair of the Board of the Australian Institute for Teaching and School Leadership. He is very well known and established in the fields of academia and education for his extensive research. His work is highly acclaimed including his books *Visible Learning* and *Visible Learning for Teachers*, a synthesis of more than 800 meta-studies covering more than 80 million students. He answers the question about retrieval practice based on his work with colleagues.

We have argued that there are five major phases in the learning cycle; Surface, acquiring and consolidating; Deep, acquiring and consolidating; and transfer (near and far).

During the consolidating phase, this is where 'overlearning' and moving from short to long-term memory is crucial, and retrieval practice is one of the more effective learning strategies (along with memorisation, distributed practice, interleaving, etc.) provided this overlearning is then used in deeper learning (and not for short-term gains, like passing a test).

Dr Jared Cooney Horvath

Dr Jared Cooney Horvath has worked as a teacher, curriculum developer, brain researcher and is currently an educational researcher at the Melbourne Graduate School of Education. Cooney Horvath authored one of my favourite educational books *Stop Talking, Start Influencing: 12 Insights from Brain Science to Make Your Message Stick* and he is a regular TES columnist. I attended the 2018 Asia Pacific International School Conference where he was the keynote speaker. His presentation was so informative and memorable, as well as thoroughly entertaining. You can follow him on Twitter @JCHovarth. Cooney Horvath offers a very useful overview of the different types of retrieval and which result in shallow or deep memories.

Memory is constructive which means the more we access and bring memories online, the deeper, more durable and easier to access in the future those memories will become. This is why retrieval practice is such a strong technique for learning. Unfortunately, retrieval comes in several different flavours.

- The most basic form of retrieval is **review:** this is where we rely exclusively on the external world to activate memories. Re-reading book chapters, re-watching lectures, and re-listening to podcasts are all forms of review as each 'activates' a memory simply by externally replaying it.

- The next form of retrieval is **recognition:** this is where we combine direct external and internal processes to activate memories. For instance, if I hand you a blank map and ask you to point to Australia, this combines effort on your part (Is it in the northern or southern hemisphere?) with direct support from the environment (It's got to be one of those shapes on the map). Multiple-choice exams, match-the pair games, and any question that includes the correct answer are all forms of recognition.

- The next form of retrieval is **cued-recall:** this is where we combine indirect external and internal processes to activate memories. For instance, if I ask you 'What is the capital of Australia?' then supply you with a guiding hint, such as 'It sits between Melbourne and Sydney', this combines effort on your part (what are some names of cities in Australia?) with indirect support from the environment (it can't be Melbourne or Sydney). Fill-in-the-blank exams, category-based game shows and any question that hints at the correct answer without directly supplying it are all forms of cued-recall.

- The final form of retrieval is **free-recall:** this is where we rely exclusively on internal processes to activate memories. For instance, if I ask you 'What is the capital of Australia?' but do not offer any hints or clues, then you are left to your own devices to dredge up the answer. Open-ended quizzes, oral exams and flashcards are all forms of free-recall.

Here's the most important bit: these different forms of retrieval each confer a different impact on memory. Can you guess which leads to the weakest and which leads to the strongest memories? As you likely guessed, review almost always leads to shallow memories that are difficult to access in the future. Recognition does slightly better, followed by cued-recall, followed by free-recall. In the end, the more effort required by an individual to dredge a memory up without external support, the stronger that memory will become.

Dr Efrat Furst

Dr Efrat Furst has a background in cognitive-neuroscientific research and her expertise is in bridging the sciences of learning with teaching and learning in classrooms. Furst designs and delivers workshops to educators to redesign classes, courses and programs. Furst supports educators with evidence-informed classroom-oriented contents and research-projects. She is currently with the Teaching & Learning Center at the Hebrew University of Jerusalem and works consulting and supporting teachers and leaders. You can follow her work on Twitter @EfratFurst.

Honestly, I think teachers who read this book already know a lot about retrieval practice, and in more than one way. As someone who's in an 'observer' position of the English-speaking teacher's community, I'm impressed and fascinated by the depth of discussion and breadth of implementation. I learned about retrieval, as a biological process involved in long-term memory manipulation, long before I learned about retrieval practice or even the testing effect, and long before I decided on my professional pathway in bridging the science of learning with teaching and learning. In fact, I believe that learning about the testing effect and realising the possible connections with the retrieval process as I knew it then, was a major turning point. Hence, I think about retrieval first and foremost as an effortful, biologically grounded cognitive process that allows us some kind of unconscious control of our vast and unimaginable memory store.

As such, it involves the activation of multiple unidentified networks and subtle interactions at multiple biological levels. What scientists do know for sure about retrieval is that it bears the potential to rewire the underlying networks and critically influence their potential to govern our behaviour in the future. Every time we attempt to reactivate a pathway, while in a different context (time, space, situation, type of cue, etc.), we integrate the retrieved knowledge with new information and feed the network with some kind of feedback that triggers a biological cascade that eventually leaves a mark. This mark, i.e. a modified network, is our ultimate goal and we have no other way to shape it. This mechanistic view of retrieval emphasises the process, its effect and the ways we can influence them intentionally 'from the outside' by inducing certain kinds of behaviour.

Retrieval practice is not just a classroom strategy, but it's a way to support the cognitive development, or reshaping neural pathways, in the brains of every student in our classes. Even if what we teach in our classes is far from simple action-response-feedback behavioural loops, some of the basic mechanisms are still relevant. Learners retrieve the knowledge as it currently represented in their brain, compare it against reality and this comparison triggers an action: strengthening, weakening or modification of the original trace.

By practising retrieval, even with the most complex or abstract material, we do two things. We reshape the pathway and we signal to the brain that this network is useful and worth maintaining. This deep connection between the strategy 'retrieval practice' and the underlying biological retrieval mechanism is what makes it so robust in my view. Moreover, this mechanistic view shines a light on what can still be discovered through research: for example, how retrieving in different contexts may shape a deeper level of meaning, or how the feedback received on a retrieval attempt shapes different networks – is it a cue to strengthen an existing mental model or rather an alteration is required, or a new model altogether. Such findings can help us refine classroom activities like using prediction before learning something counterintuitive, or how to vary and space our retrieval attempts for more meaningful processing. Such pathways of further research and refined strategies will be nurtured by a continuous dialogue between cognitive researchers and teachers and by (some) teachers thinking more like researchers and (some) researchers thinking more like teachers. I think we're already halfway there, and I'm looking forward to where this is going.

Dylan Wiliam

Dylan Wiliam is regarded as one of the world's foremost and leading education authorities. He is Emeritus Professor of Educational Assessment at UCL Institute of Education. His work with Siobhan Leahy; Embedding Formative Assessment has been incredibly helpful to educators around the world and continues

to shape practice in schools. Wiliam tweeted (2017b): 'I've come to the conclusion Sweller's Cognitive Load Theory is the single most important thing for teachers to know'. This has since been widely cited and has made its way into school policies. Wiliam informed me that a lot of his knowledge and understanding about retrieval is based on the work of Professors Roediger, Bjork and Bjork. Wiliam had this to share with teachers:

Your memory is not a hard disk. Retrieving information from a hard disk does not change the disk. However, when you retrieve things from memory that process makes the memory stronger and easier to retrieve in the future. Moreover, the harder it is to retrieve things from memory, the greater the impact that successful retrieval has on long-term memory. The best time to practice retrieving something is, therefore, just as you are about to forget it.

There is so much to take away, digest and reflect on from these great contributions. We really do need to continue to collaborate to learn and develop. Despite the different backgrounds and contexts, the academic and teaching communities are both united in their desire to provide the best possible education and opportunities for all learners. Retrieval practice is an effective method and strategy that can help us do this. I think teachers and leaders should now be considering the question: What is it students and parents should or need to know about retrieval practice?

Initially, my response to this would be, just tell them that retrieval practice works! However, based on the advice it's clear that just telling our students and their families that this strategy is effective is simply not enough. Students and their guardians need to be more informed and we have a duty and obligation to support them with this. This can be done at a classroom level with conversations happening between the teacher and their students but also at a middle and senior leader level too, with students and families. It is important from both an academic and pastoral perspective. We all have a duty to spread and share this powerful information within our school communities and decide how best to do that in our context.

I think a basic grasp of cognitive psychology and academic research is a good starting point, I do stress the basic aspect when educating students and parents about retrieval practice. Both students and parents should have an awareness of the many benefits of using this technique inside and outside of school. Finally, students and parents should be explicitly shown how to use this strategy which can include practical examples, instructions as to how to create and use flashcards in addition to knowing the importance of identifying gaps in knowledge and then using further retrieval to close those gaps, as shown in the infographic that follows.

Retrieval practice: what do students and parents need to know?

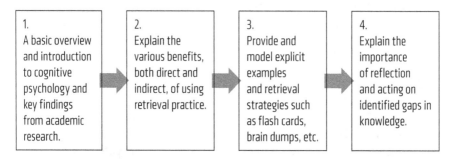

| 1. A basic overview and introduction to cognitive psychology and key findings from academic research. | 2. Explain the various benefits, both direct and indirect, of using retrieval practice. | 3. Provide and model explicit examples and retrieval strategies such as flash cards, brain dumps, etc. | 4. Explain the importance of reflection and acting on identified gaps in knowledge. |

Further recommended reading

How Learning Happens: Seminal Works in Educational Psychology and What They Mean in Practice by Carl Hendrick and Paul Kirschner (David Fulton, 2020)

Powerful Teaching: Unleash the Science of Learning by Pooja K. Agarwal and Patrice M. Bain (Jossey-Bass, 2019)

The Science of Learning: 77 Studies That Every Teacher Needs to Know by Bradley Busch and Edward Watson (David Fulton, 2019)

Understanding How We Learn: A Visual Guide by Yana Weinstein and Megan Sumeracki with Oliver Caviglioli (David Fulton, 2018)

References

Agarwal, P. K. (2019) 'Retrieval Practice & Bloom's Taxonomy: Do Students Need Fact Knowledge Before Higher Order Learning?', *Journal of Educational Psychology* 111 (2) pp. 189-209.

Busch, B. (2018) 'This is the optimum way to compile a multiple-choice test, according to psychology research', *ResearchDigest* [Online] 29 October. Retrieved from: www.bit.ly/37ud3DG

Busch, B. (2017) 'Teachers: here's how to get your lessons off to a flying start', *The Guardian* [Online] 7 June. Retrieved from: www.bit.ly/3mvTEXC

Butler, A. C. (2018) 'Multiple-Choice Testing in Education: Are the Best Practices for Assessment Also Good for Learning?', *Journal of Applied Research in Memory and Cognition* Pages 323-331

Bjork, R. A. and Bjork, E. (2019) 'Forgetting as the friend of learning: implications for teaching and self-regulated learning', *Advances in Physiology Education* 43 (2) pp. 164-167.

Bjork, R. A. and Bjork, E. (2012) 'Applying Cognitive Psychology to Enhance Educational Practice', UCLA: Bjork Learning and Forgetting Lab. Retrieved from: www.bit.ly/3aiFbvI

Bjork, R. A. and Bjork, E. (2011) 'Making things hard on yourself, but in a good way: Creating desirable difficulties to enhance learning'. In M. A. Gernsbacher, R. W. Pew, L. M. Hough, J. R. Pomerantz (Eds.) & FABBS Foundation, Psychology and the real world: Essays illustrating fundamental contributions to society (p. 56–64). Worth Publishers.

Carpenter, S. K., Pashler, H. and Cepeda, N. J. (2009) 'Using tests to enhance 8th grade students' retention of U.S. history facts', *Applied Cognitive Psychology* 23 (6) pp. 760-771.

Carpenter, S. K., Rahman, S. and Perkins, K. (2017) 'The effects of prequestions on classroom learning', *Journal of Experimental Psychology Applied* 24 (1) pp. 34-42.

Carpenter, S. K. and Toftness, A. R. (2017) 'The effect of prequestions on learning from video presentations', *Journal of Applied Research in Memory and Cognition* 6 (1) pp. 104–109.

Cho, S.-Y. (2017) 'Explaining Gender Differences in Confidence and Overconfidence in Math', *MAGKS Papers on Economics 201701*, Philipps-Universität Marburg, Faculty of Business Administration and Economics, Department of Economics (Volkswirtschaftliche Abteilung).

Cooney Horvath, J. and Bott, D. (2020) *10 Things Schools Get Wrong (And How We Can Get Them Right)*. Woodbridge: John Catt Educational.

Dunlosky, J., Rawson, K. A., Marsh, E. J., Mitchell, N. J. and Willingham, D. T. (2013) 'Improving Students' Learning With Effective Learning Techniques: Promising Directions From Cognitive and Educational Psychology', *Psychological Science in the Public Interest* 14 (1) pp. 4-58.

Gagnon, M. and Cormier, S. (2019) 'Retrieval Practice and Distributed Practice: The Case of French Canadian Students', *Canadian Journal of School Psychology* 34 (2) pp. 83-97.

Kane, T. J., Rockoff, J. E. and Staiger, D. O. (2008) 'What does certification tell us about teacher effectiveness? Evidence from New York City', *Economics of Education Review* 27 pp. 615-631.

Kirschner, P. A. and Surma, T. (2020) 'Evidence-informed pedagogy', *3-Star Learning Experiences* [Online] 21 September. Retrieved from: www.bit.ly/3nBxHr6

Knouse, L. E., Rawson, K. A. and Dunlosky, J. (2020) 'How much do college students with ADHD benefit from retrieval practice when learning key-term definitions?', *Learning and Instruction* 68.

Ladd, H. F. (2008) '3 Teacher Quality: Broadening and Deepening the Debate Teacher Effects: What Do We Know?'.

Lock, S. (Ed.) (2020) *The researchEd guide to Leadership*. Woodbridge: John Catt Educational.

McDaniel, M. A., Wildman, K. M. and Anderson, J. L. (2012) 'Using quizzes to enhance summative-assessment performance in a web-based class: An experimental study', *Journal of Applied Research in Memory and Cognition* 1 (1) pp. 18-26.

Moreira, B. F. T., Pinto, T. S. S., Starling, D. S. V. and Jaeger, A. (2019) 'Retrieval Practice in Classroom Settings: A Review of Applied Research', *Frontiers in Education* [Online] 8 February. Retrieved from: www.bit.ly/3oRWCHa

Nebel, C. (2017) 'The Big Problem with Classroom Research', *The Learning Scientists* [Online] 5 October. Retrieved from: www.bit.ly/3agnxbD

Pinkett, M. and Roberts, M. (2019) *Boys Don't Try? Rethinking Masculinity in Schools*. Abingdon: Routledge.

Sherrington, T. (2020) 'Autonomy with accountability. Implementing change from the ground up.', *teacherhead* [Online] 26 October. Retrieved from: www.bit.ly/387G3jU

Storm, B. C., Bjork, E. L. and Bjork, R. A. (2008) 'Accelerated relearning after retrieval-induced forgetting: the benefit of being forgotten', *Journal of Experimental Psychology* 34 (1) pp. 230-236.

Wiliam, D. (2017a) 'Professor Dylan Wiliam on the role of research in your classroom', *TES* [Online] 13 September. Retrieved from: www.bit.ly/3qZALzz

Wiliam D. [@dylanwiliam] (2017b, January 26) *I've come to the conclusion Sweller's Cognitive Load Theory is the single most important thing for teachers to know http://bit.ly/2kouLOq* [Tweet]. Twitter. www.bit.ly/2Ws2meN

Wiliam, D. (2018) *Teacher quality: why it matters, and how to get more of it.* London: Institute of Education, University of London.

Willingham, D. T. (2019) 'Ask the Cognitive Scientist: Should Teachers Know the Basic Science of How Children Learn?', *American Educator* 43 (2) pp. 30-36.

CHAPTER 2:
COMMON MISTAKES WITH RETRIEVAL PRACTICE AND HOW TO AVOID THEM

A question I have been asked on numerous occasions by teachers who are keen to improve their classroom practice has been, 'what are the common mistakes made regarding retrieval practice?' This is a great question as it shows a desire to improve and it also illustrates that whilst many teachers are using retrieval practice, there can be a lack of confidence about how well this strategy is being implemented and embedded in classrooms. In teaching, we do tend to go through a process of trial and error but an awareness of the potential mistakes, or mistakes others have made and shared, can help us with our practice and prevent these errors occurring in the classroom. As we know learning time is very precious.

Wiliam has written (Lock, 2020), 'As teachers, we are in the memory business. We want our pupils to remember what we are teaching. As a result, much of what happens in schools is driven by models of learning and memory that are, at best, uninformed by what research in cognitive science tells us about how learning takes place, and at worst, is actually inconsistent with that research.' This is worrying as I have seen examples of schools and individuals delivering professional development training or insets where incorrect information is being shared or there is a lack of understanding about the research being discussed and the classroom implications. This chapter focuses on a range of possible common mistakes that can be made when trying to introduce or embed retrieval practice into a classroom routine. These mistakes are based on some of my own classroom experiences in addition to discussions with colleagues and teachers. It's not always easy to discuss errors made but it is an important part of the reflection process. I have also seen resources and quizzes shared publicly where common mistakes are evident but I believe they could be easily rectified and adapted to provide more suitable retrieval challenges.

Carl Hendrick and Paul Kirschner wrote in their excellent book *How Learning Happens: Seminal Works in Educational Psychology and What They Mean in Practice* that 'retrieval practice is possibly the most effective way of retaining knowledge and yet this discovery is often used poorly in schools with testing being used as the final endpoint in a process of learning as opposed to a means of facilitating learning along the journey.' How can we ensure retrieval practice isn't used poorly in schools? A clear understanding of the basic and relevant areas of cognitive psychology is an important starting point. Then careful implementation is needed to ensure it is a strategy that becomes embedded across the curriculum with regular reflection and review.

Firstly, any teacher or school that isn't using retrieval practice is making a big mistake! The research is overwhelmingly suggestive that it is an advantageous strategy. Professor Robert Bjork has stated that 'understanding the power of retrieval practice is crucial' (University of California Television, 2016) and this is a point I repeatedly stress. As a classroom teacher and head of department, I have seen how regular retrieval practice has boosted the confidence of my students, as well as my teacher confidence, and has had a significant and positive impact on results. Quite simply, it *works.*

I am assuming, as you are reading this book, retrieval practice is an area you are keen to learn more about. I know what it is like to be promoting the use of retrieval practice in lessons when it isn't a part of the whole school culture. This is tough and was the case in a previous school. When I arrived at the school the culture focused around promoting learning styles and there were regular graded lesson observations taking place, as well as many other outdated and – at times – outrageous practices. By the time I left the school, there had been a significant shift to take a more evidence–informed approach and remove or review some of the strategies that were previously in place. Clearly, they are heading in the right direction in terms of teaching, learning and professional development. I may have only contributed slightly to that but I am glad I persevered and was never deterred.

As with everything in education, retrieval practice has the potential to be misunderstood, delivered poorly and mutated into something that hinders rather than helps learning. Professor Robert Coe (2019) published a blog post for the Education Endowment Foundation (EEF), an independent charity established in 2011 that aims to ensure young people of all backgrounds can make the most of their potential and talents, removing the barriers that come with the correlation between family income and educational achievement. Coe (2019) notes that 'there is a colossal amount of research to support the use of retrieval practice'. He further adds that 'these findings suggest that the current enthusiasm for retrieval is well-justified'. However, despite the enthusiasm and evidence, Coe does have some reservations and concerns about the implementation of retrieval practice in the classroom, making many valid points for teachers to consider and be aware of.

Coe pointed out the majority of academic research and evidence linked to this field comes from laboratory studies with North American psychology undergraduates that can, at times, gain course credits for taking part. The context to this is notably different from our own classrooms but as I stated in the previous chapter, it is not a reason to dismiss the huge volume of research available to us but it is a factor to be aware of and Coe is correct to highlight this. He argues that, in regards to the research findings linked to retrieval practice, 'there is a big difference between demonstrating this in well-controlled, small-scale research studies in which experts in the "testing effect" design retrieval activities and outcome tests and guide their use, and simply giving advice to typical teachers to incorporate retrieval quizzes into their lessons' (Coe, 2019). There is now a shift towards collecting more evidence about retrieval practice in schools and classrooms with the aim being that teachers and students will benefit from these findings in the future, which ultimately is the main driving factor behind educational research and studies being carried out.

Coe addressed some potential problems with retrieval practice when trying to implement this in the classroom. The issues raised were that teachers 'might generate retrieval questions that focus solely on factual recall (these questions are easier to generate) rather than requiring any higher-order thinking', also that 'questions might be too easy and boost confidence without providing real challenge, which is likely to be a key ingredient for generating the kind of learning hoped for' and 'teachers might allocate too much time to the quizzes, effectively losing the time they need to cover new material.' All of these points are certainly valid and many educators can likely relate to having concerns about these problems creeping into their practice. The work the EEF is currently undertaking aims to answer the questions posed by Coe as well as examine other possible pitfalls and misconceptions as well as identifying and sharing good practice. Coe (2019) stated that 'Our first few trials are as much about investigating how teachers make choices and are able to act on evidence as actually answering the impact question – no one has ever done these kinds of studies before and we have already learnt a lot about how complex they are!' These findings are yet to be released but will no doubt provide us with further useful insight in the future.

I have identified those issues highlighted by Coe, as well as other errors I have either previously made in the classroom myself or encountered and observed from other teachers. For each mistake I have offered some guidance and suggestions as to how we can avoid these to achieve significant learning gains when using retrieval practice in the classroom.

Becoming a tick box activity for lesson observations and inspections

The enthusiasm for retrieval practice by schools and recognition of this strategy by Ofsted has unfortunately meant that once again in education a strategy has fallen victim to a prescribed generic tick-box expectation. This is where we see lethal mutations or restrictions for teachers to be able to use and exert their professional judgement, expertise and autonomy in their classroom. The recognition and discussion of aspects of cognitive science by Ofsted has been warmly welcomed by many senior leaders and teachers. I do not teach in a country where Ofsted inspections are carried out but I am well aware of the influence Ofsted has on school policies in the UK and across the world in many British curriculum international schools. The 2019 Ofsted framework stated an 'important practice for effective retention of knowledge in the long-term memory is retrieval practice. Retrieval practice involves recalling something you have learned in the past and bringing it back to mind; it is far more effective than more frequently used strategies such as re-reading. Retrieval practice strengthens memory and makes it easier to retrieve the information later.' Ofsted are recognising and promoting the use of retrieval practice in the classroom, as they should be, but this reference has been enough to send some schools into panic and retrieval practice overdrive because of their fears and perceptions of Ofsted.

When we start to collect evidence for Ofsted this can impact the low or no stakes nature of retrieval and take away the many workload benefits for teachers. Clearly retrieval practice has the potential to become a data collection and analysis task to impress inspectors, which is not what it should be. Many teachers have contacted me about this issue seeking guidance. I empathise but all I can do is offer my opinions and advice. Senior leaders must be motivated by the positive impact retrieval practice has on learning rather than being Ofsted prepped and primed. Examples of where some schools have gone wrong with retrieval practice include forcing teachers to use this strategy without explaining the reasons why and the findings in cognitive psychology, therefore teachers do not fully grasp the importance and value of this technique. If the teachers do not get this then how can we expect students to?

Schools can have high expectations when it comes to implementing and embedding retrieval practice but then fail to provide teachers with enough time to learn about retrieval practice, fail to provide time to plan how to use this in lessons and within departments, and then fail to provide time to reflect on how this strategy is being used. If retrieval practice is a teaching and learning priority in a school then it should be a professional development priority too. I fully understand and appreciate the need for consistency across a school and within departments; 'consistency is key' is a continual message in this book. However, forcing and restricting each subject to carry out the same retrieval activity every single lesson every day does not factor in the nuances across different subject domains. There should be trust invested in middle leaders and teachers to embed retrieval practice into their areas of expertise, whether that be at primary level or with secondary subjects.

Only using retrieval practice at the start of a lesson

The start of a lesson is a great opportunity to carry out a retrieval or a 'Do Now' style task, which involves minimal or no instruction from the teacher as students know that upon entering the classroom there will be a task for them to 'Do Now', as promoted by *Teach Like A Champion* author Doug Lemov. Kirschner has previously stated that 'before you start something new, review the old' (Hendrick and Macpherson, 2017) and this simple advice has stuck with me to guide my lesson planning. Barack Rosenshine's (2012) 'Principles of Instruction' – which are widely referred to and recognised in schools – also encourages teachers to begin a lesson with a short review of previous learning. In my first book I dedicated a chapter to starting lessons with retrieval practice. I suggested that the best way to start a lesson is by carrying out a retrieval activity that focuses on recalling information from long-term memory based on previously taught material and I stand by this. The issue or problem isn't retrieval practice being used at the start of a lesson as it is generally agreed this is a very good way to start a lesson and can become part of the classroom routine. The issue is when this is the *only* time retrieval practice is used in a lesson. Retrieval practice is so effective it shouldn't be limited to a ten-minute task. Time needs to be dedicated to this strategy, not just the completion of the retrieval task but also time for feedback and reflection too. I am an advocate for home learning, although I am aware of the counter-arguments for setting homework tasks however, when delivered and instructed carefully and correctly, it can be another valuable learning opportunity. I often set homework that lends itself well to retrieval practice. This is something I do regularly with my classes, which can be a retrieval task itself to complete or creating question and answer flashcards to promote the use of retrieval practice at a later date.

I haven't encountered any research that suggests retrieval practice is more effective when used at a specific point in a lesson. It can be used at *any* point in a lesson. I observed a colleague in my department that delivered a retrieval task in the middle of a lesson which acted as a transition task between two other tasks and led nicely into the next section of a lesson. This wasn't anything new or radical but it was a clever approach to linking previously taught material to new content that was being introduced in the lesson. After seeing this strategy in action I have since introduced it into my lessons too. Another potential issue with retrieval tasks being used as 'starter tasks' is that this promotes the restrictive three-part lesson plan with a starter, main and plenary. The old-style plenary has well and truly had its day, or at least we hope so! The previous style of questions asked are not the questions we should be asking, such as 'what did you learn in the lesson today?' We know that time and forgetting is required to ensure the information has been transferred and can be retrieved from long-term memory. However, the end of a lesson can be a good opportunity to review the content of the lesson, to check for understanding and consolidation (as opposed to retrieval because not enough time has passed), in addition to retrieval practice with questions linked to previously covered material. An exit ticket could focus on review and retrieval. It might be worth discussing within your department or year group/phase at primary, how often do you use retrieval practice in a lesson and when? How much time is dedicated to this strategy?

Review: Summarise three main points from the lesson today.	Retrieval: Answer the three questions shown linked to previous lessons.
1. 2. 3.	1. 2. 3.

Allowing retrieval practice to hijack a lesson

I appreciate the point mentioned encourages dedicating more time in a lesson and this point may seem contradictory – do not spend *too much* time in a lesson on retrieval practice. The focus here is balance and perhaps this might be achieved through some initial trial, error and reflection. We should certainly make time for retrieval practice in a lesson but we do also have new content to introduce and explain to students. Retrieval practice is one part of the teaching and learning process, information has to be encoded and transferred to long-term memory with repeated exposure to new material and content in different ways. We can't focus on getting the information out of long-term memory if it didn't reach there through instruction, explanation and consolidation.

It has happened to me many times where a planned retrieval activity has taken much longer than I initially anticipated. Then add time for feedback discussion and before you know it this short starter task has hijacked, sidetracked and dominated your lesson. There can be a sense of panic as you didn't cover or deliver as much content as planned. My advice if this happens is to simply be flexible and adapt and plan a shorter and simplified retrieval activity to gain back some time to focus on the new material in the next lesson.

Too much focus on task design instead of question design

Task design is important, every retrieval task should be effortful and require recall. Blake Harvard (2020) sums this up beautifully as he writes: 'Retrieval practice is a mental action. It is not a specific type of activity that students do in class. It is all about students retrieving information from their memory. There are many ways this can be done.' I enjoy creating and designing new tasks for my students to complete in a lesson. I now have an extensive bank of resources, ideas and templates for retrieval practice so I can focus more time and effort into question design. Question design is of paramount importance when delivering a retrieval practice task, especially if it involves multiple-choice questions as discussed in the previous chapter. Despite its importance, question design can often take a backseat to creating and planning activities. This is where gimmickry can creep into lessons when there is too much emphasis on task design and subject content takes second place or not given the time it deserves. Strickland (2020) is an advocate for putting knowledge at the heart of the curriculum, writing that 'knowledge should carry a greater bias in curricular approaches than perhaps it does in some quarters. Put crudely, pupils simply need to know stuff'. How do we find out if learners know stuff? Regular retrieval.

A knowledge-rich curriculum shouldn't be activity led and despite sharing lots of resource templates I never felt those ideas were driving the curriculum but instead supporting and enhancing it. The subject content should be the focus and driver, with the pedagogy helping the teacher and students get to where they need to be in terms of a learning destination. Once you have an arsenal of tried and tested tasks and resources then planning time can and should be dedicated to harnessing subject knowledge and focusing on questioning. Whilst doing this we need to consider carefully what it is we actually want and need our students to learn.

The following is an example multiple-choice question, originally shared online for other teachers to use. Teachers sharing so generously is vital to the profession to help us flourish and develop. I certainly would never want to knock another teacher in the profession however, anything that is made available to the public can face challenge and scrutiny. I am well aware of this myself when I have shared a template or resource online and published books. The majority of the feedback from teachers I have received is that of praise and gratitude but there have been occasions where my ideas or resources have been challenged. When done so in a professional manner, I am grateful for this critique. It has helped me to contemplate, learn and essentially become the teacher and leader I am today. If I were to ask you who Freidrich Ebert is could you answer this? The history teachers no doubt will, but perhaps you have no idea and can't answer the question. Nonetheless, even with no prior knowledge, I am confident you can answer the question about Ebert.

Question: Who was Freidrich Ebert?

a. A bartender in a nightclub in Berlin
b. A man called Bert who liked ecstasy
c. President of the Weimar Republic

When I saw that question I had some obvious concerns. The question was for GCSE history students studying Germany 1918-45. However, as you can see, you do not need to be a GCSE historian to be able to answer that question correctly! The incorrect options are so blatantly incorrect (inappropriate too) that no recall is necessary. A correct answer can easily be achieved through the power of elimination. Evidently, the teacher was trying to be entertaining but it is simply a wasted opportunity for learning and retrieval. That specific question may seem like an extreme example but, surprisingly, there are plenty of examples like this one online that I have seen. The question could easily be rephrased and adapted, as I'll show. This could be a free recall question with no support to make it harder to generate an answer, making it more effortful and effective. Alternatively, a range of suitable multiple-choice options could be included alongside the correct answer, with options that could address any misconceptions. The issue isn't the question but more so the options provided and lack of challenge which means lack of retrieval. This is my alternative version:

Question: Who was the first President of the Weimar Republic?

a. Kaiser Wilhelm
b. Friedrich Ebert
c. Wolfgang Kapp
d. General Hindenburg

These options are more plausible. Kaiser Wilhelm was the emperor who abdicated just before Friedrich Ebert became president, Wolfgang Kapp was a political figure that led a revolt against the Weimar Republic and Hindenburg became President of the Weimar Republic at a later date. Precise knowledge of who became the first president in the context of this period is required to answer that question correctly. A distractor could also be removed as a form of differentiating the question and level of challenge. Little and Bjork (2010) have argued that when students do not know the answer to a multiple-choice question they may attempt to recall by basing it on why the other options are incorrect to reject them and help them select the correct answer. Again, we need to ensure all of the options are plausible and to provide these distractors can take time to carefully consider but, in haste, a common mistake made is to provide irrelevant options.

Question design does require the teacher to have strong and confident subject knowledge. A good idea would be to ask colleagues for feedback on the questions or collaborate. Do not spend your time designing, cutting or laminating resources and try to avoid using department meetings for admin but instead spend time thinking about the questions you will be asking your students to answer. Do you and your colleagues ever discuss questions that will be asked in a lesson? I know many departments do factor this into their departmental meetings, as Hugh Richards discussed in the previous chapter. It is a good idea for middle leaders to be aware of the questions being asked across the department. Another good idea is to network with other teachers and subject leaders from outside of your school, that teach similar content or the same examination topics, and share retrieval questions as a method of sharing good practice as shown in the following case study.

David Goodwin is a geography teacher and pastoral leader in the UK, he is very active on social media and in the online geography community. Based on the popularity of the Retrieval Roulette resource created by science teacher and head of department Adam Boxer, David assembled a team of geography teachers to collaborate and create a range of retrieval roulettes that they could all use in their lessons as a retrieval practice activity. This is a great example of teachers across different schools working together closely to create and discuss subject-specific questioning to aid retrieval.

Careful question design and collaboration
David Goodwin

The Retrieval Roulette created by Adam Boxer is a powerful tool for securing student fluency in retrieving knowledge from their working memory. On first reading, I was blown away by the simplicity and efficiency of the retrieval practice tool. Not only is it a time-saving device, but it allows for interleaved retrieval of prior learning which is something that even the most experienced heads of department will find tough to implement. I knew I needed a Retrieval Roulette of my own for my subject, geography.

During the last academic year, I began creating my own Retrieval Roulette but, having started a new role at a new school, finding time was difficult. Lockdown seemed the perfect opportunity to continue my work. Yet again, finding time wasn't easy. I knew, having created a question bank for one topic, that a geography themed Retrieval Roulette would contain more than 1000 questions. I needed a solution; I needed to share the load. In May of 2020, I tweeted this:

David Rodger-Goodwin @MrGoodwin23 · May 29
Calling all #geographyteacher who preferably teach AQA (But doesn't have to be). I want to work with a number of teachers to create a retrieval roulette for our subject like that of @adamboxer1 and the science community.
28
23
47
David Rodger-Goodwin @MrGoodwin23 · May 29
My initial thoughts are that quiz questions are created for every topic of the gcse spec (simply because that is the minimum content we will all be teaching and will have in common). Each person interested could take one topic/unit and create the relevant questions
2
David Rodger-Goodwin @MrGoodwin23 · May 29
And then all qs collated on 1 spreadsheet for our use. Depending on interest we could create more than one roulette - for individual specs etc. great way to share expertise and the workload. If interested please fill in your details on this google sheet
Retrieval Roulette
Sheet1 Name,Twitter handle,Spec taught
Fahima,@Fahima86,WJEC Eduqas A ...
docs.google.com
5
4
15

I didn't have any real expectations as to the sort of response I would receive. I hoped to have four or five teachers join me in my pursuit but, in the days and weeks that followed, I found myself inundated with messages of interest. Excited by the prospect of creating a Retrieval Roulette for geography, I set up a communal area to share ideas. My initial aim was to reduce my workload, but the result was the birth of an exciting community of 40+ geography teachers. Timesaving was no longer a priority; this project offered an opportunity for everyone involved to work with, and learn from, fellow subject experts. I knew if we were going to be successful then we would need to draw on our strengths. I asked each contributor to list the three topics they felt most knowledgeable in. This allowed me to assign topics based on the strengths of the individuals in the community, increasing the chances we would create a quality retrieval practice resource.

By the end of July, we had created two separate Retrieval Roulettes (3000+ questions) for AQA and Edexcel GCSE geography. Since then discussions have been had with different online platforms about the use of our Retrieval Roulettes and potentially turning them into apps for teachers and students to download and benefit from. I am keen for our community effort to reach a wider audience as it is not a secret there is a national shortage of geography teachers. Some schools have no choice but to appoint non-specialists to teach their geography curriculum. It is important for the schools in this situation – the non-specialists and most importantly the students – to have an effective tool for retrieval practice. I am delighted by the creation of our geography Retrieval Roulettes. Nevertheless, we continue to explore how to improve them. You will know by now, from reading this fantastic book, retrieval practice needs to be varied and so quizzes alone will have a limited effect. Currently, David Rogers (@davidErogers) is working with Kristian Still (@KristianStill), Helen Pipe (@HelenPipe1) and a small collective to develop retrieval roulettes which are more conceptual and closer to the demands of independent practice and knowledge application. They also aim to create Retrieval Roulettes for Key Stage 3 and 5.

Thank you to David for his continued professional support and inspiration. You can follow David on Twitter @MrGoodwin23 and visit his website mrgoodwin23.wordpress.com. Perhaps other subjects will now follow in their collaborative approach to designing and sharing question banks.

Question: Which of the following is the main theme of the story?

a. Superstition
b. No idea I didn't read the book
c. Banana
d. Poverty

The question above is another genuine question I found online and is based on the Willy Russell play *Blood Brothers*, often studied in English and drama. There are again two options that are obviously incorrect which can be immediately written off. According to that quiz question online, the only correct answer is superstition. It is widely accepted that poverty is a key theme throughout the play[1] so suggesting poverty is incorrect will only add

---

1   Mrs Johnstone, one of the leading characters, is poor and has to give a child away due to her dire financial situation.

more confusion. Multiple-choice questions and answers should certainly not lead to further confusion for learners but this can easily happen.

Below is an alternative version to the question, poverty and superstition remain but this again could be problematic if students answer one correct and another incorrect. A question about themes is a complex question and an even better alternative would be a free recall brain dump where you ask students to write down or discuss verbally (both from memory) the different themes that run throughout the play. If you feel that students would require some support then the picture prompt retrieval task could also be applied to this question too. Both tasks will allow for explanation and elaboration, as shown in the examples which follow. Feedback and discussion will be needed for the key themes of the play. Power and greed are not themes associated with *Blood Brothers* but they are themes in many other plays and are certainly better options than banana!

Question: Which two of the following are themes that feature throughout the story?

a. Superstition
b. Power
c. Poverty
d. Greed

Picture prompt: explain how each icon represents a key theme from *Blood Brothers*.

	Poverty and social class are themes throughout the play because Mrs Johnstone is a single mother who is poor and struggles to look after her children. Mrs Lyons is wealthy and she can give Edward a good life, he goes to a better school than Mickey and they grow up to have very different lives. The contrast is very clear.
	Another theme in the play is superstition because Mrs Lyons tells Mrs Johnstone that if Mickey and Edward ever find out they are twins then they will die. Mickey and Edward meet each other but they never learn as children that they are twin brothers. The play ends with them both dead and the narrator asks if it is superstition?
	Violence is a recurring theme in the play. This is present in Mickey's life and as he grows up we see him resort to violence and crime. Then the ending of the play is very violent with the murder of Edward.

> **Brain dump:** what are the main themes throughout *Blood Brothers*? Write what you can recall from memory below:
> Poverty and social class are themes throughout the play because Mrs Johnstone is a single mother who is poor and struggles to look after her children. Mrs Lyons is wealthy and she can give Edward a good life, he goes to a better school than Mickey and they grow up to have very different lives. Another theme in the play is superstition because Mrs Lyons tells Mrs Johnstone that if Mickey and Edward ever find out they are twins then they will die. Mickey and Edward meet each other but they never learn as children that they are actually twin brothers. The play ends with them both dead and the narrator asks if it is superstition?

These examples also show how similar questions, such as asking about themes within a play, can require different amounts of effort and explanation based on the task. A multiple-choice question will show if students can identify/recall the key themes but the free recall tasks require elaborative retrieval going into more depth and link back to the points Tomas Needham made in the previous chapter about retrieval and higher-order thinking.

Mark Enser, head of geography and author of *Teach Like Nobody's Watching: The Essential Guide to Effective and Efficient Teaching,* suggests that we should adapt the way our quizzes are created. Enser (2019) writes, 'Usually people choose questions from previous topics that have no relation to the lesson that is about to be taught. This is missing a trick. Instead, pick questions from previous topics that help pupils to recall the information they will be applying in this lesson. For example, before teaching a lesson on the impacts of deforestation I might pick questions that link to the nutrient cycle, the water cycle and development. This will help the pupils to see how this lesson connects to what they have learnt before and still take advantage of retrieval practice.' This is excellent advice from Enser illustrating how not only do we need to think about the design of the question but when we decide to ask those questions to our students. You can read more from Enser in the last chapter where he offers his advice about how retrieval practice can be applied in geography.

In addition to thinking carefully about the questions, we need to think carefully about the options we provide students and how many options are available. Two options result in a very high percentage of answering correctly without any attempt at recall with a 50/50 chance of getting the answer right – those are favourable odds! Three potential answers, where none of the options are silly or used for comedic effect, can provide a desirable difficulty for our students. Too many options can become problematic and can 'expose test takers to a lot of incorrect information, [which] is worrisome because they could potentially learn it' (Busch, 2018), which again we need to avoid.

If you have ever watched the quiz show *Who Wants To Be A Millionaire?* You will know that the early questions are worth a lower amount of money and tend to be easier multiple-choice questions. There are often options which can be ruled out instantly because it's so clearly wrong or have simply been added for entertainment value. This also gives the player that initial taste of success and a confidence boost. As the money increases the questions become harder and all of the possible options provided become more plausible. I am certainly not suggesting we take planning advice from TV quiz shows but I do think unintentionally teachers have followed the format in some ways, especially by adding a comical or random option. An example that springs to my mind is from the popular quiz show *The Chase*. There was an episode where a question was asked about the name of a fictional German cartoon character, the correct answer was Willi Wakker. The other possible options were Dick Tingler and Helmut Schmaker. It quickly went viral and was certainly memorable. This works if you're in the business of entertaining but we are in the business of teaching and learning which needs to be taken seriously, no place for Willi Wakker!

Finally, we should consider how much time we are giving students to answer multiple-choice questions. We must provide students with enough time to read and answer questions. If you are worried this may take up a lot of time in the lesson then take a 'less is more' approach with quality over quantity. Ask five questions instead of ten or ten instead of twenty – the amount of questions will depend on the question style and the context of your subject. Some multiple-choice questions have one-word options for the answers but there are also options where the choice of answers are extended sentences. Both are fine but the issue can arise when there is a timer in place. There is nothing wrong with the timer feature itself, many online quizzing tools allow you to control the timer or remove it and many provide ten seconds to read and answer a question before the question vanishes. This can be suitable depending on the content and length of the questions and options. Craig Barton (2017) suggests that in maths for diagnostic questions students should be able to answer questions in less than ten seconds writing: 'If students are spending more than ten seconds thinking about the answer to a question, the chances are that more than one skill or concept is involved, which makes it hard to determine the precise nature of any misconception they may hold.' For my subject, history, I would encourage longer thinking time, this is where subject context and expertise is key. Also, we need to consider the complexity of the question and how many distractors are included. A countdown timer with online MCQs can add pressure, encourage the student to rush, not read the question and options carefully or simply just resort to guessing, selecting any answer at random – this is not recall.

Difficulties are not desirable

I am aware how often I refer to the Bjorks but it was their superb work that coined the term 'desirable difficulties'. In a TED Talk (2018), Robert Bjork stated, 'we all have an incredible capacity to learn, the key though to recognising that capacity is to be suspicious by the sense of ease and unfettered by the sense of difficulty. In short, we need to make things harder on ourselves but in good ways'. This essentially sums up making learning difficult on purpose to ensure that the level of difficulty is desirable. I have written about this previously in both of my books and as you will have already observed it is a key theme throughout this book. The questions shown previously in the chapter illustrate how the level of challenge with multiple-choice questions must be desirable. We should provide challenges for all learners in our classes but research has suggested that younger students will need more support, guidance and scaffolding with retrieval practice (Smith, 2017).

If we consider video games, they are carefully designed to provide a desirable level of challenge for the player. Level one will start relatively easy to give the gamer a taste of success and an initial confidence boost as they progress to the next level. The level of challenge gradually increases; if the difficulty did not increase then the player will become bored. If the level of challenge is too hard that they become stuck and do not make any progress this can be incredibly frustrating and the player might simply quit the game. We are not designing games but we can provide opportunities for initial retrieval success and build the challenge keeping the difficulties desirable. Desirable difficulties can also be linked to motivation and participation with retrieval practice. Adam Boxer (2020) writes in a great blog post: 'On a motivational level, students who day after day, lesson after lesson, get questions wrong in "Do Now" activities are going to get worse, not better.' There has to be a balance between retrieval success and retrieval challenge, this is something for us to be mindful of when considering question and task design.

An example from my own classroom experience (I have shared this before but this example proved to be a turning point for me in terms of teaching and planning) is when I would present a portrait of Henry VIII on the board and ask a Key Stage 3 class to write down from memory what they can recall about Henry VIII. Some students will simply describe Henry based on the portrait. A common answer is 'he was fat'. Another problem could be students only recalling very basic facts such as 'he had six wives'. This would frustrate me as we had often gone far beyond the six wives narrative in lessons and explored the break with Rome and issues of religion yet students wouldn't recall that information. That isn't their fault, I did not specifically ask them to do so. The instructions and task itself were general and vague. This can work with older students but younger students will need explicit guidance. That specific scenario led me to create the picture prompt retrieval activity. The specific example I used with my Key Stage 3 class will follow. This involves cued recall as there are prompts to guide and support learners. There was a significant improvement in their written retrieval answers both in quality and quantity in terms of the content. The level of challenge was desirable and to pitch it at this level the answer cannot be found in academic research but instead through knowledge of our learners in front of us and the curriculum we are delivering.

Retrieval practice – picture prompt

Task: explain how each image is connected to Henry VIII and the break with Rome. Explain in your own words, from memory.

It terms of providing support and promoting challenge Cooney Horvath (2019) offers this practical advice: 'A good rule of thumb is to embrace cued recall when people are first learning new material. In this way, you can highlight the importance of associations and help others build effective association networks. As learning progresses, however, begin to pull back and move into free recall. This will ensure they strengthen associations and form truly deep memories.' This can be a scaffolding approach, providing retrieval support that we gradually remove and increase the challenge. There are things we do in the classroom, without realising or perhaps do realise upon reflection that can decrease the level of desirable difficulty. For example, the class could be answering a carefully designed question and then a student asks a question about it or the teacher simply starts a discussion and, without realising it, more hints and clues have been provided by the teacher. It can even get to a point where the teacher has ended up answering the question for the students so they now need to paraphrase rather than recall the information. Another factor that could have an impact on desirable difficulties can be classroom displays: are the answers to questions plastered around the classroom on displays that some savvy students will realise and simply be able to copy? Are class books or textbooks open and visible? Just some other factors for us to be aware of when carrying out retrieval tasks.

Bjork and Bjork have suggested a range of ways that desirable difficulties can be achieved and these include the following:

- Vary the environmental context of learning (as discussed in the first chapter)
- Vary what we chose to practice
- Space repeated study sessions
- Retrieving rather than reviewing
- Interleaving in contrast to blocking

Some of these factors are easier to do than others, depending on your context and subject but certainly spaced retrieval practice is something that all teachers can and should do to ensure learning is difficult in a desirable way.

Making it high stakes instead of low stakes

Retrieval practice has been widely referred to in academic research as the 'testing effect'. This term isn't as mainstream anymore and perhaps that could be due to the connotations of testing – appearing more high stakes.

Retrieval practice should be low or no stakes, meaning that it is low stress and unlike a high stakes final examination or test, where there is a high degree of pressure. Retrieval practice uses testing as a learning strategy, rather than an assessment strategy. I do not think teachers intentionally create high-stakes situations with retrieval practice but analysing and scrutinising retrieval quiz results, informing parents or giving rewards/sanctions are all factors that can make retrieval practice more stressful for the student.

I can remember a time in education where there seemed as if a sort of data fetish was sweeping across schools. Teachers and leaders at all levels were being constantly instructed to collect, monitor, record and analyse data. Retrieval practice can provide teachers with very useful data and insight that can inform future planning and gain an overview of class or individual progress but it should always be about the long-term learning not collecting the data and numbers. I am aware of schools reporting data and sending results from regular quizzing to students' homes. If students know their results will be collected and sent to their parents or guardians then that completely changes the stakes from low to high. As well as proving stressful for students, parents might be concerned about low scores when there may be no reason to be as forgetting is a normal part of the learning process. This is a mistake that highlights how some schools have misunderstood retrieval practice. Regular reporting and tracking of data can also become a potentially unsustainable workload issue for teachers too which can hinder the successful implementation of retrieval practice across lessons. The timer component can also add pressure and once there is pressure this impacts the low stakes nature of the quiz. Keeping retrieval regular, low pressure and low stress will have a high impact in the long term.

Lack of variation in the retrieval diet

I know teachers and leaders that disagree with me on this point, as they use the same retrieval task every lesson to promote consistency, familiarity and ensure retrieval becomes firmly embedded as a classroom routine. I do think using the same retrieval task regularly is a good thing. I remember as an NQT assuming I could only complete a task style once with a class because they had seen it before so I found myself continuously striving for the next activity to complete with my students. This was exhausting and, on reflection, there were activities I carried out that I wouldn't do now! If something works then run with it but do not limit retrieval practice to one approach. 'Vary the diet' is the phrase author and education consultant Tom Sherrington regularly uses when he discusses and explores retrieval practice in the classroom. We should provide a range of tasks and opportunities for retrieval practice, both inside and outside of the classroom. We should use both multiple-choice questions and free recall as there are benefits (as well as some cons) to using both options. We should provide students with opportunities for both verbal and written retrieval. There will be students that struggle with literacy and written communication but can verbally retrieve information quicker with greater ease. This is something for us to consider as students might not always be struggling to recall instead they may be struggling to articulate their recall in written form. From my experience, students elaborate on their answers more verbally, which I encourage them to be able to do with their written responses too.

One of the great things about retrieval practice is how flexible this strategy can be. Just some ideas include my challenge grids and Retrieval Roulette – links to both of these resources can be found at the back of this book. There are also a vast amount of online quizzing tools, some considerably better and more adaptable than others. Keep retrieval practice as a consistent classroom routine but vary the diet, mix it up from the tasks, style of recall and types of questions.

Not involving everyone in the retrieval task

This can happen in lessons without teachers being aware and this usually happens when retrieval tasks involve hands up or selecting students (either on purpose or at random) to answer questions. There is, of course, a key difference between a classroom discussion where hands up or no hands up approaches work well but we need to be mindful that if we are planning a retrieval practice task everyone should have the opportunity to recall information. Sherrington (2019) writes, 'good techniques involve all students checking their knowledge, not just a few and not just one at a time as you might do when questioning.'

I rarely allow my students to work together during retrieval tasks, that is not to suggest they cannot work together at other points in a lesson as this does take place in my classroom. However, when pairs or groups of students are answering questions then how do we know each individual has recalled that information? One member of the group (or some members) could be doing all the effort and retrieval on behalf of their peers and subsequently, this would be a wasted retrieval opportunity. This has been an ongoing problem and argument against group work.

There are tasks where students can interact with each other[2] and there are many online quizzing sites where students are grouped in teams but carry out independent and individual recall. Collaboration can play a really important role in the classroom but – in terms of retrieval practice allowing students to work with one another – it can potentially reduce the level of challenge and effectiveness of recall.

Too much focus on factual recall

Question: What year was Henry VIII born?

a. 1485
b. 1491
c. 1492
d. 1494

This question is a standard factual recall question. Key dates and chronology are important in the study of history but my question would be whether students need to know the year Henry VIII was born. Is this a key date of significance? Perhaps so, but I think being able to recall the years a monarch ruled would be more useful. This question could be useful if the other options were also key dates students were expected to know, such as 1485 was the year the Tudor dynasty was founded so that is a date students might be familiar with but can they recall the correct key events with the correct key dates? We need to think about our questions and what exactly it is we want students to know. A Knowledge Organiser, described by teacher and leader Joe Kirby (2015) as 'the most powerful tool in the arsenal of the curriculum designer', will have to require that same question. It simply isn't possible to include everything so what is it that our students need to be able to recall from their long-term memory and why? Perhaps there is a valid reason for a teacher wanting their students to be able to recall the specific year Henry VIII was born but we want to avoid retrieval practice being viewed as the ability to regurgitate random pub quiz trivia facts. Instead, retrieval practice should support learning with students being able to recall relevant information as part of a knowledge-rich curriculum. Relevant not random information is key.

Looking back to the points Tomas Needham made in the previous chapter on linking low stakes retrieval to the final examination question, I realised how too much factual recall was harming my students' work. I was marking a class set of A Level history essays

---

2   Cops and Robbers is an example of this and the template for this task can be accessed at the back of this book.

when I noticed a pattern of examples of random and isolated facts included in the extended answers of some members of the class. Although historically accurate, they were not relevant or necessary for this style of question. It was clear students were able to recall key facts in terms of dates, figures and events and were convinced they would shoehorn them into their answers. We needed to move away from this approach and this made me reflect and adapt the retrieval tasks I was completing with that class.

Viewing retrieval practice as an isolated teaching and learning strategy

This is a very common mistake I am aware of but can be easily addressed (although some strategies are easier to adopt than others). Retrieval practice shouldn't be viewed as an individual and isolated strategy to support teaching and learning. I have often heard school leaders or teachers say 'We are focusing on mastering retrieval practice then we will move onto spaced practice', but it does not and should not work that way. Another beneficial aspect of retrieval practice is that it links in so well with other evidence–informed techniques. The jigsaw puzzle that follows shows the other techniques retrieval practice can be explicitly linked and connected to, however retrieval and spaced practice are the ultimate combination for creating desirable difficulties.

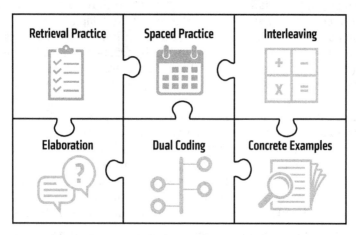

Retrieval practice is harnessing the testing effect to strengthen information being recalled from long-term memory. **Spaced practice** or distributed practice means spacing study out over a period of time rather than crammed practice. Three hours of study is better spent over a series of days instead of three hours in one session. **Interleaving** refers to mixing up subjects/and or topics instead of blocking them together. This is different from spaced practice which will be explained in more depth. **Dual coding** theory combines verbal and visual materials (this is not linked to learning styles). Information is presented in two formats to allow the information to be encoded through two different channels to memory. **Concrete examples** involve finding and using specific examples to further deepen their understanding of abstract or complex ideas. **Elaboration** in terms of a study strategy requires students to ask further questions to allow more detail, discussion and make links with prior knowledge.

I think the tendency to focus more on retrieval practice is due to it being easier to comprehend, implement and embed. Interleaving, for example, can appear complex and can certainly be tricky in terms of implementing and embedding this across a curriculum. All of the approaches mentioned promote desirable difficulties.[3] To find out more about the other evidence-informed study strategies I would highly recommend visiting learningscientists.org as they are committed to supporting teachers, parents and students to gain a good grasp of all six approaches.

Confusing spaced practice and interleaving

Upon initially discovering the science of learning, areas that I struggled to grasp most were spaced practice and interleaving. I spoke to author Bradley Busch about this and despite his level of expertise he also agreed that it can be confusing at times.[4] I know many educators that do feel they have clearly understood the concept and application of retrieval practice but do not feel as confident with spaced practice and interleaving. A blog post on the Inner Drive (2019) website reads: 'You would be forgiven for thinking, at first glance, that spacing and interleaving are the same thing: both involve leaving gaps between revision sessions on a given topic to make stronger connections. However, if you look a bit closer, you'll realise that the two study techniques are a lot more different than it seems.' Both spaced practice and interleaving are effective and retrieval practice can be stronger when combined with both of these techniques. To summarise, spaced practice refers to spreading study and recall out over time, little and often. As quoted by Bjork and Bjork (2012): 'The spacing effect is the finding that information that is presented repeatedly over spaced intervals is learned much better than information that is repeated without intervals (i.e. massed presentation). This effect is one of the most robust results in

---

3   Techniques such as highlighting and underlining were not included, where's the desirable difficulty in those tasks?
4   This did actually make me feel better as I thought it was perhaps just me. Thank you Brad!

all of cognitive psychology and has been shown to be effective over a large range of stimuli and retention intervals from nonsense syllables (Ebbinghaus, 1885) to foreign language learning across many months (Bahrick, Bahrick, Bahrick and Bahrick, 1993).' Spaced practice is also described by them as 'one of the most robust, effective ways of improving learning'.

Interleaving is where topics are mixed up in comparison to being blocked, this can be with lesson sequences, curriculum design and home study. Bjork and Bjork (2012) summarises: 'The benefit of interleaving is found over a diverse set of stimuli ranging from word pairs (Battig, 1979) to motor movements (Shea and Morgan, 1979) to mathematics problems (Rohrer & Taylor, 2007) and word translations (Richland, R. A. Bjork and Finley, 2004). Interleaving benefits not only memory for what is studied, but also leads to benefits in the transfer of learned skills (e.g. Carson and Wiegand, 1979). The theory is that interleaving requires learners to constantly 'reload' motor programs (in the case of motor skills) or retrieve strategies/information (in the case of cognitive skills) and allows learners to extract more general rules that aid transfer.'

In the same blog post from Inner Drive (2019) they explain that 'one of the main differences lies in their concepts of time. Spacing focuses on longer periods of time: for example, doing a given amount of revision over two weeks rather than cramming it all in one evening. On the other hand, interleaving concerns shorter periods of time: it's about alternating between topics during one study session ... spacing occurs between revision sessions, whilst interleaving occurs within sessions.' By interleaving topics across a curriculum instead of blocking this does result in spaced practice therefore they are explicitly linked.

Blocking and interleaving

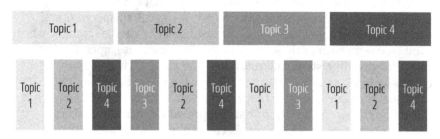

A strong understanding of retrieval, spaced practice and interleaving is essential for teachers and leaders to be able to successfully design a curriculum and sequence lessons to further support students learning long term. There were two specific examples where I listened to educators attempt to explain the concept of spaced practice to teachers and their explanations were incorrect. The first example was a webinar that I had paid to attend virtually during lockdown. During the webinar, the host told us that spaced practice involved students missing a line in their workbooks when writing to space out their work. Initially, I thought this might have been a joke, but the explanation continued on how spacing can improve written presentation and make writing more legible and visually appealing. I was muted so I was unable to comment and I would not want to heckle someone during a presentation but I found this incredibly frustrating. After the event I contacted the host and praised the specific sections I found useful. I also sent some further reading about spaced practice for clarification but the damage had been done, what if other teachers in the webinar then decided to encourage students to space out their writing hoping to see an impact on their learning and long-term memory? This was disappointing.

In another presentation I attended, the audience were told that spacing involved taking breaks in a lesson to 'space out' the learning. Suggestions were made that included giving the students five to ten minutes to chat in the lesson about any topic of their choice then return to the learning. Another option would be to provide students with Play-Doh to break up their learning. I thought my ears were bleeding; I was horrified. I don't know where on earth this information is coming from but I do think that anyone sharing best practice should have a confident knowledge and understanding of the material they are sharing with others. They have a responsibility to share and communicate accurate information. Difficult conversations are necessary as professional learning is far too important to get wrong. As a profession, we should be promoting and sharing evidence-informed strategies that are explained clearly and correctly and challenge debunked neuromyths and incorrect information – the Kirschner effect.

When I present to schools or at events I often talk about retrieval practice. I do not have all the answers but I have invested a huge amount of time and effort over recent years learning about this field. I have read extensively, listened to podcasts, presentations and reached out to experts for further support and guidance. There have been occasions where I have been asked to speak about a particular topic and I have declined because I did not feel I had the level of confidence and expertise required. In terms of professional learning and sharing,

I think it is advisable to seek people who are recommended by others and are known to be experts or well versed in the topic they will be delivering. There are certainly many intelligent and successful experts that can discuss a wide range of topics across education with ease, confidence and in-depth knowledge. However, any educator or consultant who claims they can cover it all with confidence, depth and expertise, be wary of and probably best to avoid.

Cramming retrieval practice

There are still teachers and some opponents of retrieval practice that argue there isn't enough time in a lesson to use retrieval practice or that regular testing will lead to stress. Research suggests the opposite. It suggests that regular retrieval practice can reduce exam anxiety and provide learners with a confidence boost (Agarwal, 2018). Some teachers aim to deliver all content then carry out retrieval tasks at the end of a unit or before a mock exam or real exam. By doing this we are not modelling spaced practice and not reaping the full benefits of retrieval practice. This strategy is essentially cramming with retrieval practice and this should be avoided. If you are spacing retrieval out over the academic year great. If not, then perhaps consider reviewing the curriculum and lesson plans to see how retrieval practice can be embedded and spaced out.

Not providing quality feedback and reflection time

There has been a lot of discussion on feedback, as we know this is an incredibly important aspect of teaching, learning and student progression. Retrieval practice does lend itself well to self and peer assessment. Dylan Wiliam (Hendrick and Macpherson, 2017) wrote that 'the best person to take the test is the person who just took it', promoting the use of self-assessment and reflection. Online quizzes will give students instant feedback and this is also fantastic for reducing teacher workload. However, if a student completes an online quiz scoring 13/15 but does not check which questions they answered incorrectly then they have failed to identify the gaps in their knowledge. They know there are gaps but they need to know *exactly* where the gaps are.

Putting answers on the board in front of students shows them exactly what is correct but what if a student answered a maths question wrong but fails to actually know *where* they went wrong in the process? I know I have been guilty of rushing feedback. Adam Boxer (2020) offers this advice to teachers, 'One thing you shouldn't do is to just stick the answers on the board. You want students to reflect on their work deeply, and if you put the answers on the board they won't do that.' It is very tempting to do so, especially when pushed for time in a lesson but Boxer is right, to do retrieval practice justice we need to provide time for meaningful feedback and reflection.

What is clear from all of the research I have engaged with in addition to my own classroom experiences is that retrieval practice is at its greatest when feedback is provided and reflection is used to identify gaps in knowledge. The next steps for the student and teacher should be how to close those gaps. I created a five-step study plan for my Year 11 tutor group to support them with their revision; it requires an explanation of how to create a revision list and what effective study strategies are but the feedback from students is always very positive.

Five step study plan

1. Create a list – what do you need to know?	

2. Timetable a spaced schedule.	

3. Use effective and evidence informed study strategies.	

4. Identify the gaps in your knowledge.	

5. Close the gaps. Refer back to step 3.	

Professor Agarwal (2020) has offered this advice about the importance of feedback with retrieval practice: 'Feedback helps improve students' metacognition. Without feedback, students do not know what they got correct and what they got incorrect during retrieval practice. Providing feedback is a key to powerful retrieval practice. Feedback does not mean more work for you, grading more quizzes and assignments. Simply discuss or display the answers and have students self-grade their own retrieval practice. Also, the more elaborate the feedback (e.g. with explanations), the more powerful. Learning and metacognition increase when students receive explanations about why they were correct or incorrect.'

The EEF have published their findings and reports about the impact of feedback in schools. Their website (2018) states: 'Feedback studies tend to show very high effects on learning. However, it also has a very high range of effects and some studies show that feedback can have negative effects and make things worse.' That is alarming – make things worse? Getting to grips with feedback and how we tackle this can be a daunting task but it is important and most schools do give feedback and reflection thoughtful time and consideration. In terms of reviewing the evidence, the EEF writes: 'There is a substantial number of reviews and meta-analyses of the effects of feedback. Educational (rather than psychological or theoretical) studies tend to identify positive benefits where the aim of feedback is to improve learning outcomes in reading or mathematics or in recall of information. A recent meta–analysis of studies focusing on formative assessment in schools indicates the gains can be more modest, suggesting that an improvement of about three months' additional progress is achievable in schools or nearer four months when the approach is supported with professional development.' There are many articles, blogs and books dedicated to feedback itself and it would be tempting to explore this in a lot more depth and detail however I am keen to maintain to focus on feedback and reflection with retrieval practice.

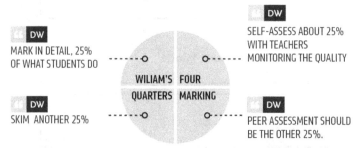

SELF-ASSESS ABOUT 25% WITH TEACHERS MONITORING THE QUALITY

MARK IN DETAIL, 25% OF WHAT STUDENTS DO

WILIAM'S FOUR QUARTERS MARKING

SKIM ANOTHER 25%

PEER ASSESSMENT SHOULD BE THE OTHER 25%.

I discovered the 'Four Quarters Marking' model by Dylan Wiliam when reading the excellent *What does this look like in the classroom?* By Carl Hendrick and Robin Macpherson. I wondered why I hadn't taken a similar approach before? I have spoken to many teachers about this with many arguing they have always taken this approach. I disagree because if that were the case there wouldn't have been as many workload issues previously linked to marking and feedback. I do think when a school adopts a specific feedback policy – whole-school or varying at departmental levels – then students and parents should be informed and understand why this approach has been adopted. A parent can often be relieved to see a tick in their child's book as this symbolises the teacher has seen their work but we know a tick or stamp does not equate to meaningful feedback.

Wiliam has offered this valuable advice to schools in *What does this look like in the classroom?*: 'In terms of what we do about this, I would say first of all, headteachers should lay down clear expectations to parents and say things like, 'We are not going to give detailed feedback on more than 25% of what your child does. The reason for that is not because we're lazy. It's because there are better uses we could make of that time. We could mark everything your child does, but that would lead to lower quality teaching and then your child will learn less. Heads have to establish those cultural norms. If a teacher is marking everything your child does, it's bad teaching. It is using time in a way that does not have the greatest benefit for students.' When it comes to feedback, communication must be crystal clear. Even if your school or department do not refer to the four quarters marking I would encourage retrieval practice to be mainly self and peer-assessed with free recall tasks being skimmed by the teacher. The other quarter, work marked in detail by the teacher should be for specific assignments, extended answers or essays but certainly not every piece of work as this is unsustainable and unnecessary.

We will need to invest time with our classes explicitly modelling and explaining how self and peer assessment/feedback should be carried out. A reason I have been reluctant to write about feedback in the past is simply that I have encountered conflicting research about when feedback should be provided. A question that is continually asked: 'Is it better to provide feedback instantly or delay the feedback and wait a short period of time?' Clearly, if using an online quizzing tool it would be foolish to ignore the immediate feedback provided. Time should be dedicated there and then to individual or whole-class feedback and reflection. There is the option for the teacher to review whole-class feedback from a quiz at a later date and then use that data to create a retrieval task to revisit the gaps in knowledge identified but generally low stakes will simply work better in the classroom when feedback is provided immediately. Busch (2016) wrote: 'The researchers discovered that in experiments conducted in a laboratory, delayed feedback were more helpful; however, in a real world setting, especially in classrooms, immediate feedback was more beneficial. This makes sense when you think about it: the real world is messy and complicated; leave things too long and things get forgotten; memories get distorted; other pressing events crop up.' There will be occasions where feedback has to be delayed, simply because it might not be possible in a lesson to dedicate sufficient time to individual feedback; not possible or practical. The research is helpful but once again classroom context is key.

I discussed whether feedback should be instant or delayed with Michael Chiles.[5] He directly informed me that 'If it is of low cognitive demand then usually it is helpful to give immediate feedback. If it is cognitively more demanding then delaying feedback can be more powerful'. In terms of low stakes retrieval practice, the majority of tasks lend themselves better to instant feedback within that lesson. Ron Berger, author of *An Ethic of Excellence*, promotes the use of peer feedback in the classroom insisting it is always kind, specific and helpful. An excellent yet simple mantra to be applied to any form of feedback. The following is an example of a simple retrieval reflection ticket I created for students to reflect on their areas of strength and identify the gaps in their knowledge.

Retrieval reflection ticket

Areas of strength/confident recall	Gaps in knowledge
• I can remember a lot of information about the Treaty of Versailles. I was able to recall the 'Big Three', the different terms of the treaty and how the German people reacted. I am confident about an exam question in this topic. • I am also good at remembering information about life in Nazi Germany, especially how life changed once Hitler came into power. I can give specific examples too about the roles of women, unemployment and propaganda. • I know the key dates, end of WWI, Treaty of Versailles, Wall Street crash, Hitler coming into power and WWII	• I struggled to remember much about the Weimar Republic, maybe because we did this so long ago? I need to go over the Weimar being established with the constitution, proportional representation and basically that time period at the beginning. • I get confused between the Sparacist uprising and the Kapp Putsch. I need to go over that again. • I couldn't recall much about Gustav Stresemann. I need to look at that again.

Failure to explain the benefits of retrieval practice to students and parents

This mistake links in with the advice offered by Paul Kirschner and Professor Tullis in the previous chapter. A research publication by Tullis and Maddox (2020) reported that more students are now using retrieval practice in comparison to previous recordings in literature.

---

5   Michael is the author of *The CRAFT of Assessment* and *The Feedback Pendulum*.

This shouldn't be a surprise considering the recent enthusiasm and interest in this strategy in schools around the world. The abstract stated that 'many students still fail to fully harness the learning benefits that retrieval practice can provide'. We need to drill down and delve deep into this to find out the possible reasons why students are yet to fully gain the retrieval practice benefits.

All schools need to be informing teachers, students, parents and the wider community about the benefits of retrieval practice which should become part of the school culture and language of learning, not just amongst staff. The infographic below suggests the main benefits of regular retrieval practice, although there are more, and this was based on the research paper by Roediger, Putnam and Smith (2011).

Five benefits of retrieval practice

1. It's a powerful strategy to support learning.

2. It can identify the gaps in knowledge.

3. Can lead to better organisation and transfer of knowledge.

4. Retrieval review is valuable for the student, teacher and parents.

5. Regular retrieval practice encourages students to study and self test more.

I have invested a lot of time and effort into this at my current and previous schools and I will continue to do so. This is an area where all teachers, middle and senior leaders, both pastoral and academic, have to work together to ensure the importance and benefits of retrieval practice are communicated clearly and regularly to students and their families. In addition to embedding retrieval practice into my classroom routines, I have also discussed this learning technique during parents' evenings, included comments about retrieval practice in written reports and communication home, as well as delivering an assembly-style presentation where all parents and members of the school community were invited, which was both well-attended and well-received. It is not always easy to get every parent on board and engaged with this information but we should keep trying to do so. Many parents are very keen to learn more about how they can support their children with their learning. We need to spread the word about the power of retrieval practice and spread it beyond the walls of our classrooms. I have also created a clear and concise study strategies guide that is suitable for parents and students, either as a hard or digital copy which you can download by scanning the QR code at the back of this book. There is no specific school branding so you could directly download my guide and share or you can use my guide as a template to create your own. I am aware of various schools around the world that have downloaded this guide and the feedback from teachers, parents and students have been very positive.

The following case study comes from Patrice Bain who I have been in contact with for about three years. She is an experienced classroom teacher passionate about applying evidence-informed strategies, like myself. In the previous chapter I wrote about research linked to retrieval practice taking place in a classroom setting and leading academics McDaniel, Roediger and Agarwal carried out research studies linked to retrieval practice in Patrice's classroom! Patrice has spent years sharing the science of learning with her students, she is now working hard to spread the science of learning with parents and in the case study that follows, she offers us some advice and insight as to how this can be achieved.

The Teaching Triangle
Patrice Bain

'Mrs Bain! I have an A (or B) in your class!' After I acknowledge this truth, the student often replies, 'But I've never done well in social studies; I always get Ds and Fs.' This is almost always followed by a common, heartbreaking student confession: 'I'm not smart.' Once again, I get the gut-wrenching realisation that my student has internalised failure by age 11. And every year, I see these same students soar and complete the year with high grades. Why? I inform the students on day one that my first commitment is to teach them how to learn. And I do. My interest in the science of learning began by chance. I met cognitive scientists Dr Mark McDaniel and Dr Henry Roediger III, authors of *Make It Stick: The Science of Successful Learning* and Dr Pooja K Agarwal. They were looking for a classroom where they could test their research. They chose my classroom and my students and I helped these researchers in their study of optimal learning conditions. I began to see why my students were learning. Little did I know that working with researchers would take my teaching skills further than I had imagined.

Our first year of research focused on the learning principle of retrieval. Time after time, test after test, the positive results of retrieval were clear. Retrieval boosts learning. In fact, the use of retrieval often improved student scores by two letter grades. Best of all, the learning was long-term. The research showed that students clearly remembered the retrieved information months later. My own research via notes and letters from former students indicate the retrieval not only lasts for months, it lasts for years! Applying the research to my classroom practice resulted in my teaching drastically improving students' retention of material. Teaching my students how to learn became a life-changer for them, as well as for me. As they mastered the methods, they soared. Students who previously felt defeated opened up to new strategies using retrieval practice, and other practices known as spacing, interleaving and metacognition, and they succeeded. We had a shared language of learning. As I became more familiar with the science of learning, I continued to develop and tweak my strategies. I co-authored *Powerful Teaching: Unleash the Science of Learning* with Professor Pooja K Agarwal which documents studies and strategies, many of those developed in my classroom.

As I worked with my students, I realised the importance of the teaching triangle: this involves the student, the parent and teacher. I had a shared language with my students but what about their parents? A particular incident hit home. A mother said to me: 'I am so frustrated because my son talks about mini-quizzes (a retrieval strategy). He doesn't do well on them and when I asked him about it his answer was "Oh mom, that was my metacognition showing me I wasn't able to retrieve it yet." What kind of answer is that?' I couldn't help but smile as I showed her his test grades: an A on every single one. After explaining the research, her reply was, 'Well how about that? He really does get it!' I realised how important it was to bring parents onboard with the value of retrieval and the science of learning. Parents of my students saw their children succeed. They began to see how the use of retrieval at home far surpassed the 'usual' homework completion in regards to scores on exams. Tests were no longer dreaded experiences but rather, celebrations of all that was learned. Discussions in the car and around the dinner table became enjoyable opportunities for retrieval.

I conducted a national survey in the United States in 2018 asking parents about learning. Here are a few of my questions, and some significant answers:

Question: What are the two top things that would help you with your child's learning? The top two answers were:

1. Understanding the basics of learning

2. Understanding how to help my child study

Question: How important is it to you that your child's teacher uses research-based learning strategies?

87% said important/very important

As I gave seminars and workshops across the United States, I was frequently asked, 'How do we have the time to educate parents about the principles of learning?' A book started to write itself in my head, which became *Powerful Teaching: A Guide for Parents*. We are truly on the cusp of an educational revolution. The science of learning – retrieval, in particular – is exploding onto the global scene. Research is accessible to teachers and parents. Science has shown us how to produce effective and efficient learning. I believe the time is here and now to strengthen the third side of the teaching triangle: Parents. Here are some questions I am hoping you will reflect on.

What if

... in the present 21st century, more students are taught how to learn?

... present and future teachers are taught methods based on research and evidence?

... scientifically proven methods are taught in professional development programs?

... teachers begin asking, 'On what research or evidence is this based?'

Ultimately the teaching triangle empowers learning at school and home. When it comes to harnessing the effects and benefits of retrieval practice it is something teachers, students and parents/carers should know.

Thank you to Patrice, as she describes herself – a veteran teacher – for sharing her experiences and enthusiasm about the teaching triangle. This is certainly an approach all schools should be considering and implementing if they aren't doing so already. You can follow Patrice on Twitter @patricebain1 and check out her website, which includes a range of articles and podcast interviews, patricebain.com.

Using retrieval practice as a punishment

Testing became almost a dirty word in education because of the negative implications of high stakes testing on students wellbeing and mental health. Regular retrieval practice has been shown to reduce stress and anxiety before taking final examinations. It is intended to be low stakes and can also prove enjoyable, satisfying and rewarding. I wouldn't blame you for thinking that retrieval practice being used as a punishment sounds absurd. I debated whether or not to include this because, thankfully, it does not appear to be common practice in schools but I have become aware of schools using detention time during break, lunch or after school to carry out retrieval practice. The arguments for this focus on detention/sanction time being used effectively as a learning opportunity. I can see the logic behind this but I would argue strongly against this approach. If retrieval practice is a punishment does it remain low stakes? How can we expect students to carry out retrieval practice independently when it has negative associations of punishment? There is a difference between using time in a detention to complete work and setting a specific test as a consequence of bad behaviour.

Assuming we know it all when it comes to retrieval practice

Clearly, this assumption does not refer to you because reading this book shows your desire to learn more about retrieval practice and improve your classroom practice. However, you may work with, lead or be led by educators that have this attitude towards retrieval practice. They understand the concept, they feel they have always implemented this in their practice and when it comes to reading any books, blogs or attending any inset presentation that focuses on retrieval practice they claim they have heard it all before. This is my second book writing specifically about retrieval practice and whilst I have an interest, knowledge and confidence surrounding this field I do not know it all and neither do I claim to do so. I haven't read every single research paper or blog post available and that is fine. As you can see through reading this book I have reached out to a wide range of teachers, leaders and experts to seek their advice and support. I will keep learning, reading and discussing retrieval practice with others to ultimately improve my classroom practice and deepen my understanding of how children learn. The concept of testing and quizzing is not entirely new in education but the wealth of information surrounding cognitive psychology that has been published in recent years and how this can be applied in the classroom is fascinating and incredibly helpful for teachers. It is far too important to ignore and the sheer volume of information available to us makes it clear no one knows it all.

It is difficult working with or talking to educators who are not willing to reflect and develop their practice. I have referred to this previously as the professional learning gap, where some teachers are flourishing by continually learning, adapting, improving and reflecting in comparison to those who argue they do not have the time or interest for professional learning and development. Teacher confidence is wonderful but teacher arrogance and ignorance is a completely different matter. Something all great teachers have in common is that they never stop learning or improving. A teacher that never stops learning will flourish in a school environment that never stops improving. A school that wants to keep on improving must have staff that want to keep on learning. When the individual teacher and school culture match in their approaches to professional learning it is the students that will benefit the most from this approach.

When it comes to retrieval practice (as with other areas of cognitive psychology) we do not know it all or have all the answers. There are further studies, experiments and research being carried out and we will continue to learn and discover more. Teachers often want black and white concrete answers but when it comes to cognitive psychology it is never that clear cut. I am often asked 'Exactly how long should I wait before I ask my students retrieval questions?' Another question asked is 'Exactly how much time shall I dedicate in a lesson to retrieval practice?' These are great questions and can help shape our planning and implementation of retrieval practice but it is complex.

Retrieval practice will take as long as is necessary for students to be able to confidently recall information from long-term memory with greater ease and confidence. I have been searching for an answer to this question and realised that this is context-dependent because of the complexity of different topics and the different learners in our classes. We cannot define an exact amount of time that should be left between new content being delivered in a lesson to when questions about that same topic should be asked, to ensure it is recalled from long-term memory, but we can estimate an optimum amount of time by knowing our classes, our subject and curriculum design thoroughly.

Further recommended reading

The researchED Guide to Education Myths: An evidence-informed guide for teachers, edited by Craig Barton (John Catt Educational, 2019)

10 Things Schools Get Wrong (and How We Can Get Them Right) by Dr Jared Cooney Horvath and David Bott (John Catt Educational, 2020)

Teaching WalkThrus: Five-step guides to instructional coaching: Visual Step-By-Step Guides to Essential Teaching Techniques by Tom Sherrington and Oliver Caviglioli (John Catt Educational, 2020)

Fiorella & Mayer's Generative Learning in Action by Zoe and Mark Enser (John Catt Educational, 2020)

References

Agarwal, P. K., Roediger III, H. L., McDaniel, M. A. and McDermott, K. B. (2020) *How to use retrieval practice to improve learning.* Washington: University in St Louis. Retrieved from: www.bit.ly/3b5zKjX

Agarwal, P. K. (2018) 'How can we reduce student anxiety?', *Retrieval Practice* [Online] 25 January. Retrieved from: www.bit.ly/3nZjXXy

Barton, C. (2017) 'What makes a good Diagnostic Question?', *Eedi* [Online] 29 November. Retrieved from: www.bit.ly/2KuaR6N

Bjork, R. A. and Bjork, E. (2012) 'Applying Cognitive Psychology to Enhance Educational Practice', UCLA: Bjork Learning and Forgetting Lab. Retrieved from: www.bit.ly/3aiFbvI

Bjork, R. A., Bjork, E. and TEDxManhattanBeach (2018) 'How to study to maximize performance', *TED* [Video] November. Retrieved from: www.bit.ly/3rOOUQt

Boxer, A. (2020) 'How to not screw up retrieval practice', *A Chemical Orthodoxy* [Online] 26 January. Retrieved from: www.bit.ly/3hjp6Hz

Busch, B. (2018) 'This is the optimum way to compile a multiple-choice test, according to psychology research', *ResearchDigest* [Online] 29 October. Retrieved from: www.bit.ly/37ud3DG

Busch, B. (2016) 'Seven ways to give better feedback to your students', *The Guardian* [Online] 10 November. Retrieved from: www.bit.ly/3nVdTPQ

Coe, R. (2019) 'EEF Blog: Does research on 'retrieval practice' translate into classroom practice?', *Education Endowment Foundation* [Online] 5 December. Retrieved from: www.bit.ly/3nGokUd

Cooney Horvath, J. (2019) *Stop Talking, Start Influencing: 12 Insights From Brain Science to Make Your Message Stick.* Chatswood: Exisle Publishing.

Education Endowment Foundation (2018) 'Feedback', *Education Endowment Foundation* [Online]. Retrieved from: www.bit.ly/2L5b8Nu

Enser, M. (2019) *Teach Like Nobody's Watching: The essential guide to effective and efficient teaching.* Carmarthen: Crown House Publishing.

Harvard, B. (2020) 'Misunderstanding Retrieval Practice', *The Effortful Educator* [Online] 26 October. Retrieved from: www.bit.ly/3rrZvRt

Hendrick, C. and Macpherson, R. (2017) *What does this look like in the classroom? Bridging the Gap Between Research and Practice.* Woodbridge: John Catt Educational.

Inner Drive (2019) 'Are spacing and interleaving the same thing?'. Retrieved from: www.bit.ly/34NoWQs

Kirby, J. (2015) 'Knowledge Organisers', *Pragmatic Reform* [Online] 28 March. Retrieved from: www.bit.ly/2JmAGVE

Lock, S. (Ed.) (2020) *The researchEd guide to Leadership*. Woodbridge: John Catt Educational.

Ofsted (2019) 'Education inspection framework', *GOV.UK* [Online] 27 September. Retrieved from: www.bit.ly/2KqGmhX

Roediger, H. L. III, Putnam, A. L. and Smith, M. A. (2011) 'Ten benefits of testing and their applications to educational practice'. In J. P. Mestre and B. H. Ross (Eds.), *The psychology of learning and motivation: Vol. 55. The psychology of learning and motivation: Cognition in education* (pp. 1-36). Elsevier Academic Press.

Rosenshine, B. (2012) 'Principles of Instruction', *American Educator* 36 (1) pp. 12-19.

Sherrington, T. (2019) '10 Techniques for Retrieval Practice', *teacherhead* [Online] 3 March. Retrieved from: www.bit.ly/3b7606s

Smith, M. (2017) 'How to Create Retrieval Practice Activities for Elementary Students', *Learning Scientists* [Online] 6 April. Retrieved from: www.bit.ly/2Jq1PHm

Strickland, S. (2020) *Education Exposed 2: In pursuit of the halcyon dream.* Woodbridge: John Catt Educational.

Tullis, J. G. and Maddox, G. B. (2020) 'Self-reported use of retrieval practice varies across age and domain'. Arizona: University of Arizona.

University of California Television (2016) 'How We Learn Versus How We Think We Learn', *YouTube* [Online] 3 May. Retrieved from: www.bit.ly/3au3ZRc

CHAPTER 3:
RETRIEVAL PRACTICE
DURING A PANDEMIC

This is a chapter I certainly never thought I would be writing prior to 2020, which was an eventful and disruptive year to say the least. Many challenges were facing the teaching profession before Covid-19 related to classroom behaviour, exam pressures, a recruitment crisis, funding and budget issues. In addition to those obstacles, the pandemic has brought about many new and unexpected challenges to the teaching profession. These are both pastoral and academic, ranging from individual to whole-school. The obstacles have led to the disruption of lessons and learning and it is not yet an issue that is resolved. We do not know when that will be or how long the effects of Covid-19 will impact our students for. I would love to have more answers and solutions but it is a time of uncertainty and we have to accept things have changed. We have to adapt, continually reflect and, most importantly, support each other. At the time of writing, there are still closures around the world and many schools continue with a form of remote or distance learning. Some schools have reopened fully but with safety precautions that include 'bubbles' which limit and control the number of people in specific areas and learning environments. Other schools have a hybrid model consisting of both lessons in schools and online. There is also the possibility of closures and further changes in the future, dependent on cases, so we would be naive to not try to be as prepared as we can in these uncertain times.[1]

There are discussions and references to narrowing and closing the Covid-19 gap and creating recovery curriculums to get learning back on track and ensure learners are not disadvantaged. We should be very ambitious and determined with this approach but ultimately this has been a global pandemic – teaching and learning have been disrupted.

---

1   Although many decisions lay outside the remit of school leaders but instead with national government policies.

We cannot exhaust ourselves trying to fix something so far outside of our control, we can only do so much. No amount of retrieval practice or any other intervention can gain back precious learning time that we lost. We also cannot tell a generation of children they need to constantly catch up. Students are well aware of the interruption to their learning and will have their own fears and concerns as parents – teachers and leaders will too. As challenging as the circumstances are, we can only continue to do our best to ensure all learners receive a high-quality education whether that is in a different classroom context or at home.

We have seen a lot of new terms and phrases used this year so it is important to establish and explain the various key terminologies. Different types of learning have occurred in 2020 as a consequence of the Covid-19 pandemic. Different schools and countries have adopted different approaches and there are some differences in the terminology used. Firstly, 'remote' or 'distance learning' refers to teaching and learning taking place outside the classroom. Not in the context of a homework or a home learning task but due to the fact students and staff cannot all be in the school building due to health and safety precautions. There is also a blended and hybrid model which involves some students in school and others learning from home or another location. There are two main types of remote learning. 'Synchronous learning' refers to students all learning at the same time but not in the same place. 'Asynchronous' refers to all students learning but not at the same place or same time.

Research has heavily influenced my classroom practice and writing as an evidence-informed teacher. This book has already explored how a significant amount of research carried out linked to retrieval practice isn't always carried out in classroom conditions and that refers to pre-Covid 19 classroom conditions too. Daniel Willingham (2020) raised a very valid point that we should be mindful of when he tweeted: 'Bears repeating: all problems in translating research to classroom practice are sig. amplified now; classrooms (live or Zoom) are more variable & unpredictable, as are students & teachers. I'd be v wary of anyone saying "research shows" about any aspect of pandemic education.'

We can certainly apply evidence and research to this new situation (e.g. continuing to use effective study strategies such retrieval spaced practice) but be mindful of the fact we do not have a body of research to rely on that is specific to the current climate.

Retrieval practice and remote learning

In the first few months of 2020, when remote learning was only considered a possibility in the near future in the UK, other countries had already had to resort to this approach in their schools. They were in a unique position to be able to share their experiences, reflections and advice. Mark Steed, Principal and CEO at Kellett School, the British School in Hong Kong, had already been leading his school in distance learning for over eight weeks in March of 2020. Steed was in a position to offer guidance to schools about how to embark on this new approach. Steed urged teachers and leaders to pace themselves and warned about the workload and staff wellbeing implications of remote learning. He wrote (2020): 'Pace yourselves: it's a marathon, not a sprint. Distance educating is tough – much harder than teaching with a class in front of you. It takes the teacher much longer to produce a video than to teach a lesson. The preparation and screen time are exhausting.' I would agree, based on my experiences of distance learning. Screen time and virtual lessons can take their toll on teachers, students and parents.

Steed further added that 'The challenge for the teacher is to keep everyone on track. There are always students who require an enormous amount of teacher input and energy to remain on task. They need no excuse to down tools at the best of times, so home learning is like three Christmases coming at once for them.' It is incredible that as a result of technology – in particular social media platforms – teachers around the world teaching in completely different continents, countries and contexts can support each other during this turbulent period. As a British teacher in an international context, closely following the decisions being made in the UK, the differences in approaches and responses I observed were very obvious. That is not to suggest that a particular country or school handled it correctly or incorrectly because everyone, from governments, teachers and leaders at all levels, were all simply trying to do the best we can for our learners. It certainly has been trial and error but a global pandemic is not the time to make an error in terms of health and safety when lives are at risk.

There were students across international schools that travelled during the holidays, to the UK and other countries around the world, but travel restrictions were abruptly introduced meaning students were unable to return and instead had to learn remotely but from another time zone. This brought additional challenges that required all to be flexible with our approaches. It wasn't just the academic aspects of school life that were disrupted but the pastoral and extracurricular too. Parents and carers had to step in and take a very active role in supervising and supporting their children, more so than ever before.

In April 2020, the EEF published *Remote Learning: Rapid Evidence Assessment* which 'examines the existing research (from 60 systematic reviews and meta-analyses) for approaches that schools could use, or are already using, to support the learning of pupils while schools are closed due to Covid-19'. The report suggested one of their key findings and implications includes: 'Teaching quality is more important than how lessons are delivered. Pupils can learn through remote teaching.' This is an essential starting point because if teachers, students and parents dismiss any form of teaching and learning during a period of remote teaching then not only is valuable learning time wasted but the Covid-19 gap will become even wider. As challenging as it can be, everyone has to take the approach and have the firm belief that, although teaching and learning will be different, learning can still occur. In terms of teaching and instruction, the EEF report states that 'what matters most is whether the explanation builds clearly on pupils' prior learning or how pupils' understanding is subsequently assessed.' A second key finding states: 'Ensuring access to technology is key, especially for disadvantaged pupils.' Technology has proven to be an essential resource for remote learning but consistency will rarely exist as children will have varying degrees of access to technology, resources and support at home. The access to technology is important for all stakeholders – the students, parents, teachers and leaders. The report states: 'In addition to providing access to technology, ensuring that teachers and pupils are provided with support and guidance to use specific platforms is essential, particularly if new forms of technology are being implemented.' It is one thing having access to technology but it is another to know how to successfully use and navigate that technology effectively.

A third key finding states: 'Peer interactions can provide motivation and improve learning outcomes.' Peer interaction is something that students have probably taken for granted in the past and this became very noticeable when learning became remote and students became isolated in their homes. When commenting on the various reviews analysed the EEF report noted, 'The value of collaborative approaches was emphasised in many reviews, although notably many studies involved older learners. Different approaches to peer interaction are likely to be better suited to different age groups.' Zoom, Google Hangouts and Classroom as well as Microsoft Teams can provide options for peer interaction and engagement. This also links to the pastoral impact of school and the noticeable absence of physical support from their peers and teachers.

A fourth key finding specifies: 'Supporting pupils to work independently can improve learning outcomes.' My own experiences of remote teaching and learning showed me that some students flourished during this period, perhaps due to a lack of distractions or increased motivation whereas other students struggled and lacked the self-motivation and discipline to study or complete work independently. My experience was reflected in a headline which read 'Remote learning has been a disaster for many students but some kids have thrived'. The article (2020) further stated: 'It has been particularly hard on children of colour, kids from families who are financially insecure, and those without access to computers and technology at home.' The EEF report (2020b) recommends: 'Wider evidence related to metacognition and self-regulation suggests that disadvantaged pupils are likely to particularly benefit from explicit support to help them work independently, for example, by providing checklists or daily plans.' Other factors can impact students working independently as there can be different distractions at home or a lack of a quiet workspace.

The last key finding states: 'Different approaches to remote learning suit different types of content and pupils.' I panicked when I initially read this because I thought some schools or teachers would interpret this as advice to use a varied range of learning styles which should be avoided even with remote learning. Different approaches certainly do not refer to a range of visual, auditory or kinaesthetic tasks for different learners but instead refers more to the flexibility required with remote teaching. Effective teaching techniques should still be used but teachers may need to adapt how they do so. The EEF report gave the example, 'using technology to support retrieval practice and self quizzing can help pupils retain key ideas and knowledge, but is not a replacement for other forms of assessment.' This advice is very sensible and, at times of crisis, common sense and clarity are needed more than ever. There can be a temptation to introduce new bold initiatives that could potentially backfire and further hinder learning. Based on the key points from the EEF guidance and my own experiences I created the infographic that follows to show how important the different factors are to teaching and learning during a global pandemic and what the potential negative impact could be when one of those factors are absent.

Teaching and learning during a global pandemic…

Retrieval practice	Communication	Access to resources	Effort/ Motivation	Support/ Wellbeing	Instruction/ Feedback	Attendance	=	Reduced disruption to learning
Retrieval practice	Communication	Access to resources	Effort/ Motivation	Support/ Wellbeing	Instruction/ Feedback	Missing	=	Gaps in knowledge
Retrieval practice	Communication	Access to resources	Effort/ Motivation	Support/ Wellbeing	Missing	Attendance	=	Lack of clarity
Retrieval practice	Communication	Access to resources	Effort/ Motivation	Missing	Instruction/ Feedback	Attendance	=	Increased anxiety
Retrieval practice	Communication	Access to resources	Missing	Support/ Wellbeing	Instruction/ Feedback	Attendance	=	Under performance
Retrieval practice	Communication	Missing	Effort/ Motivation	Support/ Wellbeing	Instruction/ Feedback	Attendance	=	Disadvantage gap
Retrieval practice	Missing	Access to resources	Effort/ Motivation	Support/ Wellbeing	Instruction/ Feedback	Attendance	=	Confusion
Missing	Communication	Access to resources	Effort/ Motivation	Support/ Wellbeing	Instruction/ Feedback	Attendance	=	Ineffective strategies

The EEF (2020a) also reported the potential impact of school closures on the attainment gap. Their main key findings were:

- School closures are likely to reverse progress made to close the gap in the last decade.

- Supporting effective remote learning will mitigate the extent to which the gap widens.

- Sustained support will be needed to help disadvantaged pupils catch up.

Again, not surprising but, of course, it is very disappointing and disheartening. Amongst the panic and anxiety teachers and students might experience we can take some comfort in the fact that we are aware of strategies that support and enhance learning; retrieval practice is one of those high utility strategies. During the period of independent study, without explicit guidance and support from the teacher, it is likely that some misunderstandings and misconceptions will need to be identified and rectified. Retrieval practice can show us what students can recall from long-term memory as well as identify those gaps in knowledge and where the misconceptions can be. Cooney

Horvath (2019) wrote: 'Ensuring there are ample opportunities to retrieve information during and between sessions will deepen memory, improve understanding and boost performance.' This advice applies and is just as relevant during any form of remote learning.

Tom Sherrington (2020) has offered advice to teachers about how to cope and adapt during this period: 'A natural tendency in these circumstances will be to set lots of independent tasks allowing students to practise and make progress at a level that consolidates and stretches as needed. But, the longer these heads-down activities progress, the more difficult it is to manage the feedback process, and we don't want all lessons to feel like a test.' Sherrington further adds: 'Use a varied range of self-check, self-quiz and peer quizzing methods to flush out wrong answers and misunderstandings. Keep in the front of your thinking: who isn't sure? Who's confused? Try to create a climate where this is totally normal and safe, avoiding making assumptions. Remember – if you focus on correctness excessively, weaker students will try to mask their problems and you really do not want this to happen at a distance when it's even easier for them to put their defences up.' The message is clear and consistent, no matter where teaching and learning is taking place, retrieval practice should also be taking place.

Technology and retrieval practice

Schools have been able to respond to the decision to launch remote learning, this has mainly been technology-based although there are specific countries and areas in the UK where access to technology at home for learning poses many problems and challenges. In the United Arab Emirates where I am based, the majority of students are very fortunate to be able to access reliable devices and a strong WiFi signal. In my current school, all students and staff are equipped with a Google Chromebook, which was introduced prior to Covid-19 with regular training and guidance for staff. There was never an expectation to use Google Chromebooks every lesson as teacher autonomy and professional judgement is highly regarded and valued. Another consideration has been screen time as we are all very mindful of the increasing screen time for many young people. However, despite the flexibility at my school to combine technology with more traditional methods of teaching and learning, following a government directive all schools across the country had to adapt to 'distance learning' – an online approach to schooling.

I work at a truly incredible school but no matter the reputation or experience, distance learning has been new for us all. We were prepared in a technological sense but there were many other aspects of distance learning that were certainly challenging for us. The lack of routine, lack of interaction with people and the change to the workload to name a few. However, we adapted and reflected regularly and never lost sight of our priorities – the wellbeing of our students (especially online safeguarding) and their learning. Retrieval practice was not something as a school we neglected. I know many teachers that already consider themselves to be very tech-savvy and have fully embraced this unique opportunity to trial new approaches to learning and explore innovative digital tools and avenues. In contrast, there are other teachers where this has been very uncomfortable and unfamiliar territory. The gap between teacher confidence using technology has existed for many years, especially with the increase of branded ambassadors roles such as Apple Distinguished Educators (ADE) and Microsoft Certified Educators (MCE) amongst others. This confidence gap has been made even more evident since the closure of schools.

Retrieval practice can take place with or without technology but the important thing is that it is taking place whether we are in a school classroom or a virtual classroom. It is simply too important to ignore. Fortunately, there are a wealth of online tools available to support teachers and students with regular retrieval practice. There can also be a range of benefits when it comes to using technology to enhance teaching and learning, especially with retrieval practice. We can and should aim to take something positive away from this experience.

I have written about the TPACCK model before, a model that I have adapted based on the work of Lee Shulman, Punya Mishra and Matthew Koehler (Mishra, n. d.). I think the concept is more relevant now than ever before. The TPACCK model focuses on balancing teacher knowledge of pedagogy, content/subject discipline, technology and cognitive science. If a teacher has strong knowledge and confidence in all of those areas then effective teaching and learning are more likely to occur. If we remove any of those factors then there will be a significant negative impact. For example, if a teacher has strong subject knowledge and can communicate that knowledge effectively using pedagogical methods linked to the evidence that informs us how students learn, but is unable to use technology efficiently during remote learning, then that will pose a very big barrier to teaching and learning. We also need to balance our professional learning so that our knowledge and understanding of each of the four areas is strong.

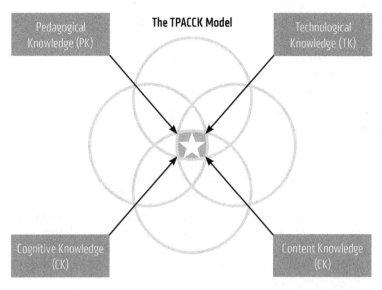

At the time of writing, my school are undertaking synchronous learning which involves 100% live Zoom lessons across Key Stage 3 classes. This, of course, is not ideal but it does help instil routines in terms of timings of the day and allows for teacher and student interaction, as well as peer interaction too. There is also a hybrid model in place where some students in specific examination years have returned to school whilst other members of the year group are attending lessons virtually from their homes. I have struggled with this concept of teaching students sat in front of me at the same time as members of the class via Zoom. A very unusual situation which has meant teachers have had to be flexible and creative! This approach is common across the country and used in other countries too. It can feel like we are a newly-qualified teacher again because we are inexperienced in this style of teaching. The key difference is that all teachers, regardless of their subject, role or experience, are in the same position simply doing the best we can. We must continue to reflect and adapt as the circumstances are ever-changing. Retrieval practice has been one of our whole-school teaching and learning priorities for the last three years, from introducing and implementing to moving towards doing the same but better. Now in regards to retrieval practice during hybrid learning, it is still a priority and we are working together collaboratively in departments and across the whole school to do so successfully but under different circumstances.

Doug Lemov (2020) has offered some advice for teachers in terms of how to master remote learning:

'1. Accountability Loops. You want to gather information on whether students are completing tasks and paying attention to the information you're sending.

2. Formative Loops. The first answer you come up with to a question is rarely sufficient. Students need to compare their answers to those of their peers to see how they're doing and incorporate new ideas to grow and develop. Discussions and Show Calls and Turn and Talks do that in a typical classroom. We want to try to provide opportunities in an online setting too.

3. CFU Loops. CFU, as readers of *Teach Like a Champion* will know, means Check For Understanding. Teaching needs to change based on the degree to which students have understood what the teacher just taught. This is even more true and even more challenging when you are teaching remotely.'

Daisy Christodolou (2020a) has written about the obstacles teachers and students face with remote learning in a blog post titled 'The challenge of remote teaching is the challenge of all teaching'. This challenge that Christodolou is referring to is that learning is invisible. She asks the important question to teachers: 'How do you get students to understand complex material, and how do you know when they have understood it?' She concludes that 'My long-term prediction about the benefits of tech remains the same as outlined in my book *Teachers Vs Tech? The Case for an Ed Tech Revolution.* I think we will always need human teachers, but I think that if used well, technology can add value. If we want technology to improve education, we have to pay close attention to what it is teachers actually do, and then work out ways that technology can support or improve those processes. Thus, for me, a discussion about ed tech is as much a discussion about formative assessment as it is about broadband access. My short-term hope is that this crisis will help accelerate our understanding of what it is teachers actually do. My short-term worry is that we end up focussing more on trying to replicate the visible surface features of a classroom and less on the invisible mental processes underpinning it.' When it comes to remote learning, whether we are simply reflecting on it, experiencing it or preparing for it to potentially happen again in the future we should never lose sight of what makes great teaching. Teaching and learning priorities should remain the same but the way we implement and embed them into lessons will be adapted based on the digital tools and resources we have access to.

Louis Everett is a history teacher and Assistant Headteacher at West London Free School (WLFS) responsible for teaching and learning. As someone who regularly advocates traditional teaching methods and has often rejected technology in the classroom, it may come as a surprise that he has championed remote learning since Covid-19 forced school closures in the UK. Louis explains his approach and reflects on his experiences of remote learning in his case study.

A teacher and leader's reflections of remote learning during Covid-19

Louis Everett

Part of my pessimism towards technology stems from my own experience of being a victim of poor use of technological innovation in the classroom as a student. The most obvious example of this is the interactive whiteboard. An array of different features added to a teacher's armoury none of which were impactful enough to outweigh the increased effort it took to write on the board. The problem with interactive whiteboards was that their use was driven by the fact the technology existed rather than in solving a particular problem: a stark contrast to the use of visualisers in recent times where a quick, efficient way to model serves a specific need that enhances traditional teaching methods. Therefore, my championing of remote learning comes out of the belief that online platforms (Microsoft Teams in the specific case of my school) solve a specific purpose at a unique time in education. The cost of students receiving no teacher instruction for what has been many months of the academic year is so great that such platforms do provide a solution. However, carefully planned implementation is needed. This case study will share our success at WLFS with the remote learning of Years 10 and 12. This has been so successful we were able to roll out remote learning to the remaining year groups after the Easter break in 2020. The reasons for this success are explored:

Simplicity and pragmatism. As soon as school closure loomed, we began preparations to use two main platforms for remote learning: ShowMyHomework and Microsoft Teams. We were keen to use ShowMyHomework as its use was already well established; almost all pupils already had access and staff were confident in its use. We chose to use Microsoft Teams as it seemed to be an effective way of delivering teacher-instruction alongside an appropriate level of interaction with students through the chat function. We encouraged departments to reject anything too elaborate and ensure the teaching and learning process was boiled down to:

■ effective teacher instruction;

■ teacher–pupil dialogue, i.e. questioning for comprehension and retrieval practice; and

■ student application and teacher feedback.

This was the starting point for all departments. If they then wanted to break out, we ensured they had the time and space to do so. However, just because the technology exists, it does not mean it's a good idea to use it. We honed in on what would be most impactful and rejected what would be ineffective and distracting.

Subject-specificity rules so empower departments. As an SLT we established the three-point framework mentioned then handed it over to departments. We utilised external training from Microsoft and gave concise training only on the basic functions of the platforms rather than trying to be too intricate. We gave departments as much time as we could to prepare, freeing up time within the school day and clearing time after school by cancelling unnecessary meetings, training or events. This time, space and clear brief empowered subject-experts to utilise the technology in the best way for their subjects. Consequently, departments came up with innovative solutions to subject-specific problems; the maths department prioritised taking visualisers home, the English department made use of Microsoft's Shared Notebook and our classics department marked PDF live for Latin translations.

Create a buzz around sharing practice. I wanted to share good practice without being prescriptive. I asked departments to share their 'Teaching and Learning Tips for Remote Teaching' and collated this into a document I updated daily and sent out every morning whilst we remained closed. Each 'top tip' had a description which recognised the teacher's contribution and explained why it was such a useful strategy. This recognised teachers' achievements whilst providing support for adapting to remote teaching. It was also a useful way of controlling the quality of remote teaching through positive reinforcement of simple, high-impact strategies. The document helped staff devise solutions to the unique problems remote learning poses. For example, our divinity department shared the strategy of giving all pupils time to type an answer to a closed question in the chatbox before pressing 'enter' simultaneously to gauge whole-class understanding. Lots of departments submitted strategies to tackle the problem of increased workload when feeding back remotely. I was able to collect strategies together, linking them to manageable chunks of theory and then distribute them as part of our headteacher's daily update.

Don't try to replicate the school day but do attempt to sustain a sense of community. Initially, I thought there would be an abundance of time created by the lack of commute, duties, detentions, extra-curricular activities and so on. However, the differences between teachers' home lives, the emotional strain of Covid-19 combined with the workload that comes with transferring to online teaching meant replicating the school day would be unwise. Therefore, we decided to start with only teaching Years 10 and 12. We have now decided to teach Key Stage 3 with just one lesson a week for each subject (two for core subjects) where essential concepts and processes are prioritised to cut down on workload for teachers and pupils (see my next point for more detail). Despite this, I would stress the importance of trying to sustain a sense of school community to benefit teachers, parents and pupils.

Our headteacher sent out lighthearted and uplifting daily updates which included essential messages from each SLT member combined with the sorts of anecdotes and messages that bring a school community together, such as sharing emails from parents, praising excellent lessons and thanking individual departments and teachers. Her annual Founder's Day speech was recorded and circulated to parents, pupils and teachers with a similar aim. After Easter, we started to distribute assemblies weekly to intensify this. Perhaps the biggest indicator of the importance of the school community has been student and staff attendance of remote lessons that have been well above our predictions. It seems the interactive capacity of Microsoft Teams to keep teachers regularly in contact with one another and pupils has been important during these uniquely challenging times.

Use interactive time for essential concepts and processes. Remote teaching is difficult. Lots of the weapons within a teacher's armoury are removed (e.g. eye contact and other non-verbal signals). The submission of work and providing feedback are also more time-consuming. However, one of the reasons I'm an advocate of remote teaching during these difficult times is the importance of direct instruction and pupil-teacher dialogue for any learning to take place in addition to regular retrieval practice. Asking students to learn without this is hopeless. Think carefully about how you use interactive (teaching) time most effectively and think about how pupils can then consolidate this independently. For example, in history we are ensuring we read extended text aloud to students, then stop for teacher instruction with the use of visual aids with moments built-in for comprehension questions and consolidation as well as some modelling of the writing process. Then students are given a series of writing tasks to complete independently. This is an excellent opportunity for schools to think about what makes effective use of lesson time. One of the common pieces of advice I give heads of department who ask how to fit in all content as part of their GCSE courses is to focus on selecting familiar, high-impact tasks that illuminate the inherent interest within topics. In reality, if the task cannot be achieved over a platform like Microsoft Teams, it might have been overly complicated and distracted from the inherent interest in the topic.

Daisy Christodoulou wrote an excellent blog (2020b) which helped me in preparing for school closure in my SLT role of teaching and learning where she argues that 'the challenge of remote teaching is the challenge of all teaching'. Her argument that remote teaching should be more a discussion of effective teaching generally rather than online teaching specifically, in our experience was true. If you are in a situation where you are preparing for remote teaching then tread carefully, but also confidently with a clear sense of what good teaching looks like. Platforms like Teams enable teacher instruction and pupil-teacher dialogue to continue to ensure that independent work completed can focus on retrieval, space-repetition and practice. A transfer to remote learning has been an opportunity to prioritise high-impact effective teaching methods whilst cutting away distracting gimmicks to improve teaching overall.

Thank you to Louis for sharing the process of teaching and learning in 2020 experienced by staff at WLFS. You can follow Louis on Twitter @LouisEverett1 and read more on his teaching and learning blog justonethingafteranotherblog.wordpress.com.

My success criteria when it comes to using technology for retrieval practice follows. Stick to this rule of three and you will likely find the right online tools to support your teaching and your students' retrieval.

Retrieval practice with technology checklist

Low stakes – Does the online tool provide opportunities for low stakes quizzing/retrieval?

Workload friendly – Will the online tool support your workload with low effort, high impact?

User friendly – Is the online tool user friendly and easy to navigate for both the teacher and student?

If you are sharing or recommending a website or app to colleagues before you do so check it suits the criteria mentioned in the graphic and these factors are likely to encourage others to engage with the technology too. Another additional point – not one I consider to be essential – is the flexibility of the quizzing tool. Does it allow for both MCQs and cued or free recall? I tend to use different types of online tools for different types of testing for example, I will tend to use Quizizz on a more regular basis for low stakes retrieval practice but in regards to a formal type of assessment, I will use Google Forms. This can help to make the distinction between low and higher stakes testing.

I also only use free quizzing tools because there are so many great options that do not cost but a lot of online quizzing sites have more features available with an upgraded version at a cost. During Covid-19 some edtech companies provided free or discounted software for schools to support them with remote learning as a goodwill gesture. It is worth exploring the resources that are now freely available for schools.

The following are five online tools that I recommend, in no particular order, which can be used for retrieval practice, whether that be at the start of a lesson, as part of an online remote lesson or as a home-learning task. They vary from MCQs, cued and free recall. All of the suggestions below pass my success criteria as they are low stakes, workload friendly and user friendly.

Adam Boxer is a science teacher and head of department who I have referenced throughout this book as his presentations and blogs have proved most helpful. I always find his work interesting and useful. A retrieval resource that Adam created and shared online for other teachers to use was Retrieval Roulette, as discussed in the case study in chapter 2 and which I also explored in my previous book. Building on the success and popularity of Retrieval Roulette a digital version Carousel was created. Adam writes about this exciting new website that teachers across all subjects and age ranges can use to regularly implement retrieval practice into their lessons.

Carousel Learning

Adam Boxer

The Retrieval Roulette was a great program, but it could only get you so far. If you were looking for a way to embed retrieval into your day-to-day practice, it was the perfect tool in generating questions for you, either from the distant past or from more recent learning. However, retrieval in class is only a fraction of the battle, and in truth, classroom experience tells us that the time and effort students put in at home is what makes the real difference. Sadly, for work at home, the Roulette could not quite do the job. I tried everything I possibly could: I gave students dedicated exercise books for retrieval homework, took them to the computer room and showed them step-by-step how to use it, made a video for parents explaining how to use it, publicly praised students who were taking it seriously and hauled up those who weren't. It was always a losing battle: every additional click in Excel is an additional point for a student to get stuck and immediately give up, and that's just among the students who managed to even open it to start with. Many of my students didn't have access to a laptop and were understandably struggling to work it on their phones or small tablets. Others had laptops but didn't have Office. An upgrade was desperately needed.

It is at this point that Carousel comes in. Josh, Jose and I wanted to build something that could not only replicate the Roulette but also give it a significant power-up. We wanted a program that:

■ could work on any device.

■ be completely student-proof.

■ assisted teacher workload with automatic marking.

■ enabled the sharing of best practice through community question banks.

■ kept track of students' responses over time through a markbook.

■ enabled teachers to drill down into student knowledge with advanced data analytics.

■ allowed us to research and incorporate sophisticated algorithms that adapt to students' forgetting curves.

■ got students and teachers excited about retrieval.

Now, every single one of my classes gets a Carousel quiz a week. It takes me about two minutes to set it and I'm guaranteed quality student work in response. When I mark a quiz and scroll down the list of responses, I can see effortlessly the students who get it, the ones who do not and – perhaps most importantly – the ones who think they get it but really don't. Then, I can skip straight to the big picture and see which topics my students struggle with most, which areas I can quickly rectify and which will require a more serious re-teach. As far as promoting and keeping track of retrieval – and, therefore, learning – over the long term, Carousel is by far the most powerful weapon in my armoury. The best thing about it is that we are still growing.

With over 3000 early adopters signed up, we have a huge community of teachers who are giving us high-quality feedback to help us improve Carousel. We have some genuinely revolutionary features in the pipeline and, as time goes on, hope to continue growing into a one-stop-shop for the research-informed teacher.

You can follow Adam on Twitter @adamboxer1 and visit his fantastic teaching and learning website achemicalorthodoxy. wordpress.com. Carousel is brilliant because it is a digital retrieval tool created and based on an idea by an evidence-informed teacher. To find out more visit: carousel-learning.com

Mentimeter

Mentimeter is great for low stakes (essentially no stakes) retrieval for a variety of reasons. It is a website (Mentimeter.com) that I found myself using a lot during online distance learning. It is free but there are limitations and opportunities to upgrade to a pro account. I have managed well with just the free version. It serves as a presentation tool and although I only use it for retrieval tasks, I know colleagues and other educators that use Mentimeter to combine their lesson slides and retrieval questions. This site allows the teacher to create a presentation where different questions can be included. The main reason why I like Mentimeter so much is due to the variety on offer. It allows teachers to combine free recall opportunities with open-ended answers and multiple-choice questions. The quizzes can be shared with others via link or QR codes and results can be downloaded or reset.

In addition to the retrieval style questions, other features can also be used in a lesson in both the physical or virtual classroom if all students have access to technology. It is possible to create a collaborative 'Word Cloud' as a class. This can be done by asking the class to use three adjectives to describe an individual, event or concept studied. Words that are repeated then appear larger in the Word Cloud. There is also an option to rank answers and use a scale for questions that are linked to retrieval but instead could be 'How far do you agree/disagree?' There is another feature to rank answers too and a Q&A function which allows students in the class to submit a question.

Students go to Menti.com and type in the code on the teacher presentation, which can be accessed using any device. Mentimeter really is low stakes – students do not need to login or even submit their names, making the answers truly anonymous. Consequently, Mentimeter is better for gaining a whole-class overview and other options such as Quizizz would be better if you wished to be able to view specific individual data and results. The thought of students submitting answers anonymously might fill some with dread but there is a profanity filter and the teacher controls sharing answers with the rest of the class. For genuinely low stakes retrieval quizzing online Mentimeter is a good option.

Quizizz

I have written extensively about Quizizz previously. The reason I continue to write about this quizzing tool is that over the years it has continued to expand, develop and adapt to teachers' needs. This progression is due to Quizizz actively seeking out teachers – myself included[2] – to gain their perspective. The CEO Ankit Gupta actively invites teachers to provide feedback and insight so this resource can continually adapt and improve to support teachers and learners. Personally, Quizizz ticks every box. The following is a summary of some of the excellent features on the basic plan which requires only an email to sign up.

The **teleport feature** allows teachers to search through other quizzes and teleport whole quizzes or individual questions to a new quiz. Once teleported, the teacher can adapt the question or distractors. This is great for teacher workload although I advise you to be careful as not all publicly available questions have been designed carefully. **Instant feedback** is provided to students. The reports provide a useful overview of whole-class and individual progress for the teacher. There are options to **personalise quizzes** by adjusting and removing music, question timers, memes (or create and upload your own) and the leaderboard. Quizzes can be set live in a lesson or as a homework assignment with a **deadline date and time**, which is useful for asynchronous learning (there is also a two-week limit on quiz deadlines but I don't think that is an issue). There is the option for an **instructor paced quiz** which allows the teacher to control the pace of the quiz. Students can **compete in teams** where they can answer individually at their own pace but their scores are grouped within their team.

---

2   I am not endorsed by Quizizz and I am not an ambassador. I simply rate this site very highly.

Quizzes can also be **linked to other virtual learning platforms** such as Classroom or Teams. There is the option to provide **multiple choice questions, polls, fill in the blanks or open-ended free recall** and the option to **insert images, audio clips and maths equations.** Quizzes can also be **shared with other colleagues,** which is great for collaboration across a department. Quizizz has a lesson function where you can **create or import slides and embed quizzes.**

Anki

Flashcards are a firm favourite for me when it comes to retrieval practice. I recognise they have their limitations and there is a skill in creating effective flashcards but they do work across all subjects and can be used with the recall of facts, dates, quotes, definitions and more. They are a very simple technique for learners to use: low effort in terms of creation (when spread out over time) but high impact in terms of long-term learning. As well as being an effective learning strategy, flashcards also tend to be very popular with students. Miyatsu, Nguyen and McDaniel (2018) found more than 50% of college students reported they use flashcards to study. We need to take care and be cautious when it comes to encouraging and instructing our students to use flashcards. They can be an effective technique but that depends on *how* they are used, *when* they are used and *what* content is included. Pooja K. Agarwal (2019) has observed that 'Lots of students use flashcards. But using flashcards doesn't guarantee they're using retrieval. In fact, students could be wasting their time'. My mantra is that flashcards do not need to be flashy; a simple question on one side and answer on the other.

The main purpose of flashcards should be self-testing to strengthen information in long-term memory and provide instant feedback to identify gaps in student knowledge, not re-reading cards over and over again. A collection of colour-coded flashcards with detailed notes and diagrams filling each card are not worth the effort and time they take to create. Students will spend hours transferring information from a textbook to a flashcard which does show students are revising, investing time, effort and energy into their studies but often they are simply copying their notes onto cards and re-reading. We know these are not the most effective study techniques, so it is important students know this information too. When students use flashcards that contain a question on one side and answer on the other (or keywords and definitions on the back) this promotes self or pair testing ensuring active recall – retrieval practice is actively taking place. It is vital students include the answers when creating flashcards because this provides the necessary instant feedback and guidance. This feedback also informs students as to what they need to return to and focus on. Using flashcards for testing is simply the best and only way to effectively use flashcards.

It is important that students consciously recall the answer to the question on their flashcards, either verbally or through writing. The reason for this being that many students can struggle to self-test. They may see a question and think or assume they know the answer and, before consciously recalling it, they have turned over to read the answer and told themselves they knew it. In reality, they just recognised the answer instead of going through the retrieval process. Cheating is easy too so self-discipline is required. Students should say the answer out loud or write the answer down before checking. It's not difficult to grasp, but it's surprising how flashcards can be used in different ways, impacting how effective they are as a learning strategy. Retrieval practice is most effective when combined with spaced practice and flashcards can combine both techniques. I am keen to share information about how flashcards can be used effectively with parents, as Patrice Bain advocated in the previous chapter with the teaching triangle. I also want to encourage younger students to use flashcards, which I know many primary schools have successfully implemented and embedded. Flashcards tend to be created using index cards that can be purchased in most stationery shops but recent years have seen an emergence of apps and websites that allow students to create their own or use existing digital flashcards. A flashcard app I will be suggesting that teachers, students and parents try is Anki.

I often recommended a range of apps and websites that can be used for digital flashcards. One website that is now standing out above the rest is Anki. A free flashcard tool that uses sophisticated software to promote spaced retrieval practice. Users can create their own flashcards or refer to a bank of premade flashcards decks that can be downloaded. The app states it has over 80 million flashcards available but you can whittle that down through a specific search otherwise that would be overwhelming! The flashcards can include text, sounds or images, therefore it is great across a range of subjects and has been recommended by MFL and music teachers.

There will be a question or prompt the student will answer then flip the card and can rate their answer from fail, hard, good or easy so students must be honest when doing so. Anki can record and monitor progress. Using the results and its unique algorithm it will prioritise the following questions asked based on the gaps in knowledge and to ensure spacing occurs. Anki can be used across devices, including the Cloud so students can use the app across different devices if they wish to. It is still early days for Anki but it is very exciting and they have stated they are keen to develop this app further based on feedback from learners and teachers. Try out Anki and if your students are searching for a digital flashcard option then this would be a very good recommendation.

The flashcard process, whether it is digital or not, should involve the following stages:

Flash cards for retrieval practice

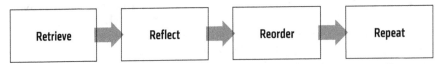

Flipgrid

Flipgrid is not known for being a retrieval practice resource but it can be used for that. There are three reasons I wanted to include Flipgrid in this chapter. The first being that it has been highly recommended to me by lots of teachers who use it in their own lessons, and even more so during remote learning. Secondly, Flipgrid provides opportunities for verbal recall, linking back to varying the retrieval diet. Thirdly, Flipgrid allows for peer collaboration, interaction and feedback which I know is something many students have missed during isolation.

Students can access Flipgrid from any teacher and once the teacher has set up an account, grids are created which essentially serve as virtual classrooms. There is the option to select school email so that students can only join a grid/class using their school email or there are other ways to ensure privacy and safety. Colleagues can also be added to a grid as a co-teacher. Once assignments are set, students record themselves speaking and upload it to the grid. This allows the students to complete a verbal brain dump, instead of writing everything they can recall from memory they do so verbally. This can be related to a specific question or topic. There is an option for the teacher to provide written or verbal feedback. Peers can watch each other's videos and provide feedback and commentary. There's a host of features and lesson materials that can be collected and customised; primary and elementary teachers have told me Flipgrid is very user friendly for younger children and they have loved the opportunity to watch and listen to videos of one another whilst outside of their normal classroom environment. There is also the option to put a limit on video recordings, as some students we know can talk for a long time! Flipgrid has certainly grown in popularity during remote learning and there are a vast amount of tutorials via blogs and videos available online to support teachers getting the most of this online learning tool.

Socrative	Seneca Learn	EdPuzzle
Google Forms	Edmodo	Pear Deck
Quizlet	Kahoot	Plickers
Nearpod	Google Jamboard	Padlet
Microsoft Forms	Gimkit	Remembermore.app

The table above shows a range of additional online low stakes quizzing tools that can be used for retrieval practice inside and outside of the classroom. Whilst I do not use all of these quizzing tools, these recommendations are based on my own experiences and conversations with colleagues and teachers online. Each quizzing tool has its pros and cons and we all tend to have some go-to websites that we like and can rely on for low stakes regular retrieval practice.

Remote retrieval routines

Remote lessons are simply not the same. For the majority, remote lessons are not as enjoyable and don't feel as effective. Although remote learning is not preferable it does not mean that it cannot be high quality. Below are some of my tips for remote learning and keeping routines in place. I have noticed how much students crave routines and it helps them to stay motivated and organised throughout the school day.

- Keep retrieval a regular part of lessons, it can be used at the start of a lesson as students are joining a virtual lesson they know to immediately join the online quiz. It can be frustrating when students arrive at a virtual lesson at different times, often slow internet is blamed or they may just be struggling to be organised with timekeeping as there is no school bell at home to tell them break or lunchtime is over! Just because a lesson is shorter or virtual does not mean we cannot provide time for feedback and reflection.

- Low stakes is more important than ever, as some students are really struggling with the current situation so high stakes testing can further add to that anxiety.

- Keep the learning platforms the same across a school, for example all classes should use one platform whether that be Google Classroom or Microsoft Teams, just keep it consistent. Parents have spoken to me about this, when their children are uploading work to different platforms from Google Classroom to SeeSaw or using Zoom then Microsoft Teams for virtual lessons. It's a confusion everyone can do without. However, with low stakes quizzing we can use a variety of quizzing tools with ease. There are plenty of choices available. A student might go from lesson to lesson using Kahoot throughout a school day and that will become repetitive.

- Continue to work with colleagues and share quizzes that are created. This will support consistency across classes but also collaboration is great for workload, especially as we are adapting our curriculum to ever-changing circumstances.

- Retrieval practice can allow students a screen time break. Time away from screens is so important, for students and teachers! If students have a pen and paper at home (they will only need basics) then they can complete a brain dump style task. They can spend a short amount of time writing what they can from memory. This does not need to be shared with the teacher as it is no stakes but this requires a lot of trust! We know some students would take this opportunity to take a little break so I have only tended to do this with older students. Students could simply hold up their paper responses or take a photo and upload, both in terms of accountability and for the teacher to see an overview of their recall.

- Focus on prior existing knowledge but you will need to drill down on prerequisite knowledge – information students need to be able to access the lesson content and material.

It can feel like we are in limbo at times, remembering life pre-Covid-19 and planning for life and normality to return post-Covid-19. There are lots of uncertainties about this time but one thing is clear is that life has changed globally and each individual is trying to navigate and find their own 'new normal', both inside and outside of the classroom. As teachers, we adapt to different situations daily and, once again, we are adapting and rising to the new challenges faced whilst remembering this is not a time to simply keep children busy at home but ensuring effective learning is still taking place.

Jodie Powers is a middle leader at John Taylor High School (home of the Staffordshire Research School) and SCITT lead for geography at the

National Forest Teaching School. Jodie has written the following case study on some different approaches we can take and factors we should consider when attempting to close the Covid-19 gap in schools.

Closing the Covid-19 gap in schools

Jodie Powers

'Unprecedented times' – two words which were used repeatedly in 2020, especially as shorthand for the societal upheaval brought about by Covid-19. One of the most fundamental changes experienced was the closure of schools. UNESCO estimates that, globally, 1.5 billion school-age children have been deprived of a classroom education since the onset of Covid-19. For teachers, the closure of schools has posed a host of challenges, but the gradual re-opening of schools has been no less problematic. When – if at all – will we return to the 'old normal'? Will there be yet more changes to the examination system? Will ITT (Initial Trainee Teacher) students be expected to launch themselves into full-time teaching as an NQT, despite their training year – a crucial year in the development of any teacher – having been cut short? These are just a few of the vast array of questions that we will be required to answer in the coming month and possibly longer.

The EEF has published its rapid evidence assessment on the impact of the school closures on students. Their overwhelming conclusion is that the closures are likely to reverse progress made in narrowing the attainment gap in the last decade. Perhaps, then, the most important question posed by the reopening of schools is this: what can teachers do to bridge the attainment gap between disadvantaged pupils and others, which has only been widened by Covid-19? Retrieval practice will be one of many key factors that are essential to close that gap.

Positive relationships:

Whilst we have interacted with students via email, Zoom and/ or Microsoft Teams, remote learning can never be an adequate replacement for classroom-based learning. Online we can't take social cues from students about their understanding of the content, peer over their shoulder to correct errors or develop depth in understanding, nor can we pick up on their feelings. When students return to school, it will be vital to reinforce relationships between teachers and students. Doing so will, firstly, help students regain confidence and enjoyment in learning, and, secondly, will encourage students to put behind them the stresses and strains of living in lockdown. Inevitably, some of our students will have experienced bereavement and all of them will be sorely deprived of social interaction with their friends and peers. Take time to get to know your students for the first time or once again.

Diagnosing misconceptions and gaps in learning through retrieval practice:

Whilst many of us have spent hours scaffolding and modelling remote learning resources, they are simply not as effective as face-to-face teaching. Subsequently, our second key focus should be on identifying student's misconceptions or knowledge gaps. An effective way to do this is through retrieval practice. The diagnosis of these gaps and misconceptions needs to be subtle: students will be facing enough stressors as it is without the impression that they have fallen behind being reinforced in every lesson. So announcing to students that they will have a test in October on everything they covered the previous year is probably not the best way to diagnose these gaps or begin the process of re-building student confidence. After the gaps and misconceptions have been subtly identified, future planning and consolidation activities can be targeted at rectifying them, reinforcing retrieval practice's primary use as a teaching tool over an assessment tool.

Setting effective homework:

The third key element is effective homework. The EEF have indicated that effective homework can add up to five additional months of progress at secondary level and two additional months at primary. Homework has to assist students in progressing. It is not enough to ask students to revisit topics which have been taught remotely at home. In fact, doing so will inevitably reinforce gaps and misconceptions. The use of low stakes quizzing or consolidation activities such as concept maps can be used to ascertain gaps, or students could be asked to RAG rate their understanding of the different elements of a topic. Not only can these quizzes be highly effective when structured well, but as they are also self-marking, you will be able to manage your workload and that of your team. Where possible, make use of technology such as Google Classroom or Microsoft Forms to identify knowledge gaps through homework, and use the results to inform your retrieval practice and starting point for teaching at the start of the next lesson.

Developing self-regulation and metacognitive skills:

Finally, even though we may have been out of the classroom for a long time, we have to remember that *we* are the experts. Our subject knowledge is our strength. We are best placed to show students how to be effective learners and how to be successful in our subject, overcoming the challenges they will inevitably face. The EEF's 'metacognition and self-regulation' summary of recommendations shows us that we need to be explicit as experts in our rationale for utilising strategies such as retrieval practice, as well as modelling our thinking to help students develop their metacognitive skills, which allows students to become more successful learners as they understand more about how they learn. Furthermore, linking back to the previous point, homework can also incorporate metacognitive activities such as modelling how to complete exam questions.

All of the old challenges we face as a profession will remain, not least adjusting the curriculum yet again. However, we must remember, first and foremost, that we are classroom practitioners, regardless of our position in the school hierarchy, and that the return to classroom-based learning is a good thing. We entered the profession to help the next generation succeed in our subjects and their education. Consequently, ensuring our classroom practice is the best it possibly can be is ultimately the only way to close the attainment gap that Covid-19 has amplified.

Thank you to Jodie for sharing excellent pieces of advice that are useful as we continue to work through this new phase of schooling and getting back on track. You can follow Jodie on Twitter at @MissPowers_Geog

It's easy to view 2020 and 2021 as doom and gloom but we have to try, as difficult as it might be, to find those silver linings in life with teaching and learning. There have been some benefits of remote and hybrid learning. Many teachers have embraced this opportunity to rapidly upskill their tech skills and knowledge during this intense period. We have all certainly learnt a lot and are likely now much more familiar with online tools and platforms that perhaps we did not use before or nearly as often.

2020 was a great year for online professional development. Teachers, leaders and academics around the world have been so generous sharing their time and wisdom to support educators. I was watching a superb researchEd presentation delivered by Paul Kirschner (researchED, 2020) where he said: 'We are in a war zone at the moment, we're not doing our best to save lives but save learning and save children.' This struck a chord with me about how important our role has been in 2020 and how well we have all done coping with the new challenges and demands. As a profession, we have always known it was never our job to set online tasks just to keep students busy or preoccupied instead the focus has always been on saving teaching and learning.

Teaching and learning have also been captured online and not in a way that focuses on teacher scrutiny or as an inspection evidence collection. Students can rewatch explanations, instructions and feedback provided by their teachers through video. There are probably lots of children around the world who had previously wished they could press pause and rewind during a lesson and now that is possible. This has been a time where creativity has flourished both with students and teachers in terms of the work produced. Technology can provide solutions to some of the workload challenges facing the profession, for example, online quizzes that score and record the results for teachers or digital questions banks being created by teachers for other teachers to use and contribute to.

This is temporary and when we do return to school fully (whilst the effects and impact will no doubt be long-term and we will have to deal with a transition phase) there will be a new appreciation for the school day, routines, interactions and much more. Remote learning has given both students and teachers an increased sense of gratitude towards school. The first break time duty I completed in school, with children in the building, after six months of remote learning felt very emotional for me. It made me realise how much I had missed so many aspects of school life that before I took for granted or even complained about! For a lot of people, the past year has changed their perspective in regards to many aspects of our lives, both professional and personal.

Before schools rush to spend money or introduce new and elaborate interventions to catch up or close the Covid-19 gap, it is worth remembering retrieval practice is a low cost, low effort and high impact strategy, whether that is in a virtual or physical classroom. It is one of the strategies we can harness to save teaching and learning.

Further recommended reading

Teaching in the Online Classroom: Surviving and Thriving in the New Normal by Doug Lemov (Jossey-Bass, 2020)

Teachers Vs Tech? The Case for an Ed Tech Revolution by Daisy Christodoulou (Oxford, 2020)

Education Exposed: Leading a School in a Time of Uncertainty by Samuel Strickland (John Catt Educational, 2020)

Education Exposed 2: In pursuit of the halcyon dream by Samuel Strickland (John Catt Educational, 2020)

The researchED Guide to Leadership: An evidence-informed guide for teachers, edited by Stuart Lock (John Catt Educational, 2020)

References

Agarwal, P. K. (2019) 'Make flashcards more powerful with these 3 tips', *Retrieval Practice* [Online] 18 November. Retrieved from: www.bit.ly/3hr5qBA

Christodoulou, D. (2020a) 'The challenge of remote teaching is the challenge of all teaching', *Daisy Christodoulou* [Online] 6 April. Retrieved from: www.bit.ly/3aTfkdU

Christodoulou, D. (2020b) 'Remote learning: why hasn't it worked before and what can we do to change that?', *Daisy Christodoulou* [Online] 14 March. Retrieved from: www.bit.ly/3n3ycJw

Cooney Horvath, J. (2019) *Stop Talking, Start Influencing: 12 Insights From Brain Science to Make Your Message Stick*. Chatswood: Exisle Publishing.

Education Endowment Foundation (2020a) 'Best evidence on impact of school closures on the attainment gap', *Education Endowment Foundation* [Online] 12 June. Retrieved from: www.bit.ly/34Tq6gr

Education Endowment Foundation (2020b, April) *Remote Learning: Rapid Evidence Assessment*. London: Education Endowment Foundation. Retrieved from: www.bit.ly/3rvRFGe

Guastaferro, L. (2020) 'Remote learning has been a disaster for many students but some kids have thrived', *Washington Post* [Online] 3 October. Retrieved from: www.wapo.st/37Wtw3M

Lemov, D. (2020) 'Mastering remote teaching– Intro: two types of learning', *Teach Like A Champion* [Online] 18 March. Retrieved from: www.bit.ly/38Hj7bD

Mishra, P. (no date) 'TPACK', *Punya Mishra's Web* [Online]. Retrieved from: www.bit.ly/2WQs7FQ

Miyatsu, T., Nguyen, K. and McDaniel, M. A. (2018) 'Five Popular Study Strategies: Their Pitfalls and Optimal Implementations', *Perspective on Psychological Science* 13 (3) pp. 390–407.

researchED (2020) 'researchEDHome 2020 Paul Kirschner: Ten Tips for Emergency Remote Teaching', *YouTube* [Video] 2 May. Retrieved from: www.bit.ly/3rFRc4n

Sherrington, T. (2020) 'Teaching from behind the safety line..', *teacherhead* [Online] 17 September. Retrieved from: www.bit.ly/3pAjXoK

Steed, M. (2020) 'Covid-19 Advice for School Leaders: Pt7: Pace Yourselves', *LinkedIn* [Online] 31 March. Retrieved from: www.bit.ly/34RprfB

Willingham, D. T. [@DTWillingham] (2020, October 12) *Bears repeating: all problems in translating research to classroom practice are sig. amplified now; classrooms (live or Zoom) are more variable & unpredictable, as are students & teachers. I'd be v wary of anyone saying "research shows" about any aspect of pandemic education.* [Tweet]. Twitter. www.bit.ly/34QtlVK

CHAPTER 4:
RETRIEVAL PRACTICE WITHIN EACH SUBJECT DOMAIN

I have taught a wide range of subjects throughout my career but history is my specialism. As I have written about the importance of retrieval practice within each domain, I thought it would be useful to include a discussion of what retrieval practice looks like in the primary classroom, as well as across a range of subjects studied at secondary. It simply would not be right for me to write how retrieval practice should be specifically applied in different subjects as I do not have the depth of understanding and classroom experience necessary to give each subject the justice it deserves. Instead, I have enlisted a wide range of teachers and leaders that have expertise in their subject domains. The *crème de la crème* from EduTwitter and superb teachers I have had the privilege to work alongside. The educators range from classroom teachers, middle leaders to senior leaders. Each one of them has applied retrieval practice in their subjects – implementing, embedding and reflecting. I am delighted to be able to share their words of wisdom in this book.

I believe the golden nuggets of advice below will be useful for classroom teachers, heads of departments and senior leaders with responsibility for line managing different subjects across the curriculum. What does retrieval practice look like in each subject? As an aspiring senior leader myself, I can appreciate how an awareness and understanding of the nuances of retrieval practice across the different subjects is incredibly important and helpful. I certainly didn't tell anyone what to write. I provided everyone with the opportunity to discuss retrieval practice in their subject, as you will see some teachers have shared their own journey and approach to retrieval practice whereas others offer more practical advice and classroom examples. More discussion with retrieval practice within specific subjects is required. Often general research and resources are shared and teachers are told to simply adapt and apply. We need to discuss and share with colleagues and subject communities how we are adapting and applying retrieval practice in our subjects.

Primary education

Jon Hutchinson

When I first started teaching in primary, my planning process was what I would call 'activity-focused'. When given the topic for the next half-term, I would begin by thinking about the activities that pupils could complete. Teaching Roman Britain? Get them to paint some shields and practice standing in the turtle formation. Doing volcanoes in geography? Make sure that you have plenty of PVA glue and strips on newspaper – it's time to paper mache! Writing a fantasy story in literacy? I saw on Twitter that you can make it look as though a dragon is terrorising the playground, let's do that! I worked like this for years, and the children seem to have lots of fun in my lessons. Feedback from observers was pretty good, and parents were happy their kids were enjoying themselves. The only problem (and it is quite a big problem) is that it gradually dawned on me that my pupils didn't really *know* anything that we were ostensibly learning about. They could paint a red and gold roman shield but they wouldn't be able to tell you much about the Roman Empire, it's greatest and most terrible emperors, how it rose, or why it fell. That sort of thing. And since pupils aren't generally tested formally in many of the foundation subjects in primary, they were able to happily move through school never really learning anything at all.

I thought that this wasn't good enough. It didn't align with my values of wanting all children to achieve academically, regardless of their background. It wasn't fair that in my classroom, the only way you could learn stuff about the Romans was if you went home and learnt about it from your parents. It quickly dawned upon me, as well, that many of the things that I most prized in the classroom – creativity, critical thinking, enquiry, collaboration, diverse thought – were all grounded in having a well-developed schema, furnished with lots of knowledge. Put simply, you cannot critically think about the Romans if you don't know anything about them. So a while back I made the move to a knowledge-based curriculum. That term, now, has become unhelpfully politicised and may well cause a wince or a cringe. All I really mean by it is that I start by planning what I would like my pupils to know, not what they will be doing. The first unit that I undertook this new approach with was the Apollo 11 moon landing. I created a knowledge organiser with a list of all of the facts that I wanted pupils to know by the end of the unit, which I would hold myself accountable for. There were about 50 in all, things like Neil Armstrong being the first person on the moon, that they said 'The Eagle has landed' when their lunar module first touched down, that the USA was engaged in a space race with the USSR – that sort of thing.

When I showed this to colleagues, many of them were shocked at the expectation, which they considered entirely unreasonable. 'How on earth can you expect seven year olds to remember all of that?' I pointed out that many of them, and many of those who we referred to as our 'lowers' were perfectly capable of learning the names, positions and goal records of the players in their favourite teams. So why shouldn't they know as much about the topic they are learning about at school? I was a bit worried though, especially as I was still a new teacher. Maybe it was unreasonable. How wrong I was. Over the last five or six years, one thing has become abundantly clear to me: children in primary school *love* doing retrieval practice. There must be something about the clarity and the sense of accomplishment that makes it so appealing, as well as the fact that it is bite-sized and gives immediate feedback. We started by covering up one column in the knowledge organiser at the start of each lesson and filling in the blank gaps to see how many facts we could remember (for example, if one column had Bull Aldrin, then pupils had to write 'Lunar Module Pilot'). This was a great way to engage parents too as they can easily become involved with their child's learning, making sure that they know everything that they need to to be successful in their lessons and retain the knowledge in the long term.

As time went on, we became a bit more creative. In the first lesson of each unit we will make flashcards using the knowledge organiser. Pupils can use these to quiz themselves at spare moments in the day, as well as at home. Many of our pupils use the Leitner System (moving flashcards into boxes which will be saved until a later day) to ensure that they are spacing their retrieval. Flashcards can also be used to do a quick partner task, turning it into a game. There are also several websites which allow us to transform these retrieval questions into online quizzes that can be completed both independently and whole class. In lessons, we quickly saw the difference. Pupils could authoritatively and clearly discuss the topic, using rich and specific language and technical detail. Writing became much easier for them as well, as they knew so much and their limited working memories could focus on constructing the best possible sentence, not wondering about what to write. The achievement gap, too, appears to be narrowing, as all pupils have the same, clear expectation set out for them and teachers know exactly what they need to make sure all children know. Retrieval practice in primary really is a game-changer, so much of what we care about can be supercharged by having the children engage in it. If you haven't already, I strongly recommend that you give it a try.

Jon Hutchinson (you can find him tweeting as @jon_hutchinson_) is Assistant Headteacher at Reach Academy Feltham. He has taught across both Key Stage 1 and Key Stage 2 and also tutors on Ambition Institute's Masters in Expert Teaching. Jon has sat on expert panels for the Department for Education, Ofsted and the Standards and Testing Agency.

English

Jennifer Webb

English encompasses two separate but inexplicably linked subjects. We might define English language as the study of how to read critically and write effectively. English literature is essentially the study of the written word as art. They are different in focus but profoundly reliant on one another. There is a common myth among students (and some teachers) that you cannot revise for English language and that English literature revision is just about 'learning quotations' to use in an examination. This misconception has come about because, in examinations, both subjects rely heavily on writing and on reading unseen texts. People believe that you cannot prepare for reading or writing by knowing 'stuff'. This is not true.

English language

Language is composed of words and their semantics, syntax, punctuation and grammatical structures. The best writers are the ones who know lots of words, who know the rules for using punctuation correctly, and who know how to apply grammar accurately to create precise meaning. This is content which can and must be taught; students with such content at their fingertips can write with fluency, intelligence and precision. As teachers of English Language, we can use recall strategies to support: vocabulary growth, such as regular spelling tests; quizzes for definitions; recall of synonyms for key terminology;

quizzes for semantic history, etymology and morphology; and word webs (where students link together words with the same roots, prefixes or suffixes). We can also teach grammar and punctuation rules and reinforce this learning with quizzing and free recall activities.

Writing is a skill, but it is built on a bed of knowledge. Mimicry leads to habit, which leads to independence. Students can be taught phrasing and sentence patterns to copy in their own writing. If they learn how a well-constructed sentence sounds and feels and they commit such structures to memory, they are then able to use this knowledge to compose excellent writing independently. We can provide students with a range of phrasing, such as sentences using: 'the more... the more... the more...' as a rhetorical structure.

English literature

The study of literature involves an enormous amount of content. Students must be able to recall information about: text plot and character detail; the historical, literary, social and religious context of texts; literary theories and the history of text reception; key themes, motifs and ideas inherent within texts; literary devices – what they are and how they can create meaning; literary symbolism; literary form and structure. And, on top of all this, yes, they need to 'learn quotations.' There are many ways of using recall in the literature classroom; quizzing, dual coding, 'brain dumps' and free recall are incredibly effective and can be used meaningfully for any literary knowledge in any age group. Another very helpful strategy is group chanting: students memorise quotations or chunks of text and practise reciting that content during lessons or as part of their personal revision. This is particularly helpful because, in the case of poetry and drama texts written in verse, students can gain a sense of the rhythm and performance power of the lines they are learning. I have used this technique to get students to memorise entire Shakespeare soliloquies with students as young as Year 7, and this has always supported student understanding of texts and their confidence in writing about them independently.

Across all of English, recall is a powerful tool to promote ambitious knowledge, creating a foundation for great writers and independent readers.

Jennifer Webb is an English teacher and author of *How To Teach English Literature: Overcoming Cultural Poverty* and *Teach Like A Writer*. Jennifer regularly delivers subject-specific CPD for teachers, as well as being the keynote speaker at various high profile educational events. You can follow her on Twitter @funkypedagogy and find out more by visiting her website funkypedagogy.com.

Maths

Ben Gordon

Spaced retrieval practice is an essential element of the teaching and learning of mathematics. I have never understood the 'drill and kill' vs the 'teach for conceptual understanding' argument. It is a false dichotomy. Conceptual understanding without fluency means that students' working memory is more likely to overload while trying to remember the basics, leading to a lack of or ineffective problem-solving strategies. Students who try to solve a problem with fluency but no conceptual understanding often fail with applying their skills to unfamiliar problems. Developing conceptual understanding improves storage strength (encoding) – an important aspect of the learning process.

The learning of mathematics is made up of learning facts, concepts, processes and problem-solving strategies. Regular spaced practice which induces strategy selection when looking at different concepts and processes is important. We can start with planning. The lesson is the wrong unit of time in terms of planning for regular retrieval. Teachers should plan which mathematical ideas we return to over a period of time, namely a learning episode. When students are revising independently, they should plan the ideas they are going to review over a block of revision sessions in advance rather than sitting down and taking one session at a time. This will increase the opportunities to develop retrieval strength over time. Where facts are to be learned, self-quizzing using flashcards is a useful strategy. Students can make this more effective by using the Leitner system. This could include command words, definitions, key formulae or develop question stems that support strategy selection. For example, 'when I multiply a negative number by a positive number the result is...'

The choice of an appropriate strategy is often difficult because superficially similar problems sometimes require different strategies (e.g. Chi, Feltovich and Glaser, 1981; Siegler, 2003). This is where it is important to make teachers aware of how we can improve what is perhaps the simplest principle of learning: the practice of a skill improves the performance of that skill. This is where the research behind interleaved vs blocked practice is of benefit in mathematics education, which is now more developed in our subject than most others and one of Bjork's desirable difficulties. A guide to this and its application to mathematics was published by Rohrer, Dedrick and Agarwal (2017).

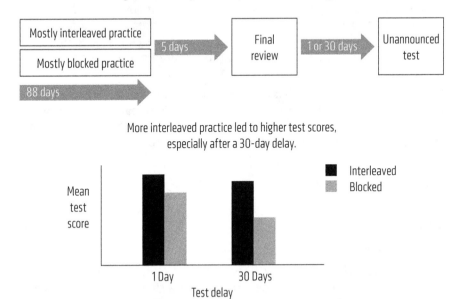

The findings are that students who receive mixed practice exercises following instruction on a certain topic outperform students on an unannounced test quite sometime in the future. The reason? If you teach Pythagoras' theorem when finding the hypotenuse of a right-angled triangle and then provide an exercise of 12 questions that only test this then there is no strategy selection involved. This would be classed as blocked practice. We can develop this a little further by introducing questions that involve students applying the theorem to find one of the shorter sides. Furthermore, we could introduce problems involving right-angled triangles that do not involve applying Pythagoras' theorem – problems involving angles, similarity or area. Interleaving is much more effective where related ideas are taught and tested in close proximity (McGrane and McCourt, 2020).

This must not be confused with spaced practice – exercises that involve completing different problems that are maybe not related ideas. This is still certainly more beneficial than blocked practice but providing tasks and resources that induce fluency synthesis through interleaving, over a period of time, will ensure that students become more proficient in not only recalling what to do but when to do it. Teachers can apply this tomorrow by thinking about the mixture of practice exercises they give to their students when several related ideas have been taught either in the classroom or at home. Having solutions available for multi-step problems is of benefit as it takes the focus away from the solution and more on the method but also ensures that students can self-regulate against the correct material, an essential requirement of effective retrieval practice.

Ben Gordon is Assistant Headteacher and Curriculum Area Leader for maths in Blackpool. Ben regularly delivers CPD to teachers and leaders and he is maths SLE. You can follow him on Twitter @mathsmrgordon and visit his blog teachinnovatereflectblog.wordpress.com.

Science

Gemma Singleton

As a science teacher I have always felt the curriculum was packed with knowledge. I have seen numerous cohorts sit examinations, each requiring the skills to retrieve, apply and link significant knowledge. Within science, we have numerous forms of knowledge, which can pose an additional challenge in securing this within our learners. Skills and understanding are seen as forms of knowledge and sometimes it can be perceived that there are no generic skills that can be taught outside of the specific factual knowledge required. Knowledge can enable learners to feel powerful and increase their confidence within science but acquiring this knowledge cannot be left to chance. We need to think of accessible and creative ways to really develop retrieval practice and retain the key knowledge needed to be successful, which should drive and underpin our philosophy and curriculum.

The quantity of knowledge required in science can be overwhelming, so being specific about what the specific knowledge we need students to learn is imperative. We require students to have more than a general sense of things. To really acquire knowledge, students need to know the details and make the synoptic links between the scientific concepts to reinforce learning, developing their own schema and to aid retrieval. Our learners can gain significant tacit knowledge through the experiences we provide, but we must also consider the declarative and procedural knowledge that is also essential to their success. These aspects need to be considered when looking at a unit or sequence of lessons so that as teachers we are covering the detail needed for success. Below are some strategies to support this:

Concept	Strategies to use in the classroom
Begin lessons with a review of previous learning	Retrieval Roulette, low stakes quizzing, recall tasks, exam questions, tell me what you know activities. Open-ended tasks remove the limitations of what students can achieve. The goal free effect is successful in science as it does not restrict the learner and provides the opportunity for you to see how the learner thinks and their retrieval capabilities. An example of how to use this effectively in science is presenting a graph for students to tell you what they know about the data presented to them, rather than limiting this to 'Describe what happens' or 'What pattern can you see?'
Present new material in small steps incorporating student practice	Breakdown concepts, chunking, summarise-restate-discuss, effective assessment of learning after each section, broken down exam questions, structure strips. The use of the visualiser aids the presentation of new ideas as it enables you to model your thinking as the expert, for students to see how to approach tasks, questions or challenges and is supported by effective questioning to check understanding. An example of this would be introducing the carbon cycle in steps and explaining each organism's role and process as you move through the cycle.
Limit the amount of material a student receives at one time	Introduce in small steps and identify key learning over quantity. Overloading information can be detrimental due to the limited cognitive processing capacity, so when providing students with information – particularly procedural information such as a practical or experimental method, it is important to introduce in small steps, so students can learn to retrieve correctly.
Clarity in instruction and explanation	Think aloud, model the steps, simple and concise, introduce meaning to new terminology (word roots/decoding), dual coding – using visuals, visualiser, annotate exam questions on the board. Science, like most subjects, is full of complicated words, steps, cycles and processes which can become evermore complicated if the clarity of instruction and explanation is missing. The use of the visualiser to model can support clarity. This is further supported by dual coding and the use of images to enable students to gain an understanding of what is happening. For example, when teaching about the immune response in biology, the use of images enables students to see how the different white blood cells function as well as work together.

Questioning is key – vary the types of questions to check understanding	Check responses of all students and provide systematic feedback with corrections. Types of questioning include hinge, diagnostic, probing, cold calling, no opt-out, think-pair-share, say it again but better, whole-class response. Questioning is a fundamental tool to assess retrieval and understanding of knowledge. However, this is not just applied in learning verbally. Cold calling, probing questions and checking for understanding does have its place in a lesson, however we can also be creative to get more input from more students at any one time. Retrieval quizzes and grids are a staple of my lessons and happen at multiple points throughout the lesson. Silent self-quizzing is also important and supports students' confidence as they can reflect on their answers privately. The key to questioning and quizzing is regularity as this supports the retrieval process between the long-term and working memory.
Provide high-quality practice for students, and guide them as they begin	S.L.O.P booklets, independence booklets, exam questions; try to develop fluency. Practice is important and this needs to be deliberate. Focused activities and questions on the core knowledge and facts need to be regularly practised and retrieved. An example here could be when I teach photosynthesis. I will start with retrieval questions every lesson and build this into homework with variations of the questions being asked. I will also provide goal free material surrounding the structure of a leaf and the limiting factor graphs to enable students to show what they know. I would also include at first very structured questions linked to the practical work associated with this topic around testing a leaf for starch and how light intensity affects the rate of photosynthesis. I would then start to build in longer answer questions to enable students to retrieve the stages in the practical. Retrieval and S.L.O.P booklets are also used throughout the year to enable students to offset the forgetting time.

Gemma Singleton is Assistant Headteacher and a science teacher at Meridian High School. You can follow Gemma on Twitter @MrsSingleton and visit her blog meridianhigh.wordpress.com.

Religious education

Dawn Cox

One of the biggest challenges for learning and retrieval in RE is the time between lessons. With a lesson a week or every two weeks, getting students to remember the last lesson's learning can be tricky.

A quick quiz at the start of the lesson can help to recall prior learning to get students back into a topic. Keep it simple, no stakes and allow a high success rate to give students confidence. Choose questions that help link to the content for the current lesson, so that the sharing of correct answers acts as the lesson introduction to save time. As we study different religions and beliefs that are seemingly unique, when introducing a new topic we need to make as many links to prior learning as possible. Making connections allows students to recall prior learning and gives them a 'peg' to hang new learning. In RE this may be key concepts that go across religion and beliefs such as 'sacrifice' or 'prayer'. At GCSE level, students need to know relevant quotations to support their points. One way to support learning these from the start is to teach them in context and then quiz students on them regularly. This can include giving quotations with words missing to fill in or giving them a topic and asking them to identify a relevant quotation.

For classes that are taught infrequently, using homework for retrieval is a good use of time. Learning keywords, quotations or substantive knowledge by quizzing is accessible for all students by giving students a technique to do it, e.g. self-quizzing using a knowledge organiser or making and using revision cards.

Dawn Cox is an experienced teacher of RE and leader. She is a regular blogger, sharing classroom practice and reflections to support others. You can follow Dawn on Twitter @missdcox and visit her blog missdcoxblog.wordpress.com.

Geography

Mark Enser

We are fortunate, in many ways, that we teach geography. One reason for this is that the powerful pedagogical principle of retrieval is embedded in the very structure of the discipline. We teach a naturally synoptic subject in which several sub-disciplines are brought together to do geography. We may break our programme of study into topic blocks, moving from urbanisation and tectonics to development studies, but we should always be aware that their learning of one topic should influence their study of another. This then becomes a rich opportunity for retrieval practice. For example, when studying the 2015 Nepal earthquake in a topic on tectonics, pupils may be asked to retrieve what they had learnt during their work on urbanisation to help explain the high death toll in the capital. They might do this in a quick quiz at the start of the lesson in which they have to retrieve key words and ideas from that previous topic or through the activities they do during the lesson in which they have to recall their knowledge on the causes and effects of urban sprawl.

We can even make sure that these opportunities for retrieval practice are planned for in these prior units. The work on urbanisation could use the Nepal earthquake as an example of why urban planning is necessary, ready for them to revisit and retrieve during the next topic. The topic on tectonics could lay the groundwork for an understanding of development studies that will then be retrieved and used during the subsequent topic. As with so much else, retrieval as a pedagogical approach is a curriculum planning issue and in a topic like geography, with its focus on bringing disparate knowledge together, that could not be more exciting.

Mark Enser is head of the geography department and research lead at Heathfield Community College. He is a regular writer for the TES and has authored *Making Every Geography Lesson Count, Teach Like Nobody's Watching* and co-authored *Fiorella & Mayer's Generative Learning in Action* with Zoe Enser. You can follow Mark on Twitter @EnserMark and visit his blog teachreal.wordpress.com.

History

Kate Jones

I considered asking a history teacher to contribute because I know so many brilliant history teachers online and in person but I wanted to unashamedly take the opportunity to write about two things I am passionate about combined: retrieval practice and my subject!

Hugh Richards' case study in chapter 1 offers a superb explanation as to how retrieval practice can be implemented in the discipline of history and I will aim to simply add to that. A lot of the research and studies carried out linked to retrieval practice have tended to focus more on subjects such as mathematics and science but we know retrieval practice is essential to the study of history and has been warmly welcomed in the history community. History teachers have embraced retrieval practice but the misconception that students might make in terms of retrieval practice and history, is that this simply involves lots of factual recall of key dates and individuals. As a history teacher, it can be tempting to rely heavily on multiple-choice questions. However, we *must* use regular free recall in history to move away from regurgitating key dates but instead allow opportunities for elaboration and wider debate and discussion. Also, we need to be careful how much support we provide and striking the balance can be difficult. A typical chronological sorting task will contain a lot of prompts in comparison to students recalling events from memory in the correct chronological order but a free recall timeline can also be very challenging too. An alternative would be to provide students with a timeline and then they fill in the gaps of key dates and events from memory, or to allow recall and elaboration we can provide students with a completed timeline where they have to verbally recall or write down what they can about a selected event from the timeline. We need to make the level of challenge desirable.

When designing questions we need to carefully consider the significance and relevance. We don't want students to write extended written essays that are littered with isolated and random key facts that focus more on a descriptive narrative rather than getting to grips with and tackling the demands of the question, this is especially true at A Level. Students simply will not be able to recall everything we teach them so we need to drill down and focus on the core elements students need to know. In terms of dates, terms, individuals, events, causes, effects and more – what are the essentials that students really must know? Then we can shape our retrieval tasks around that. Strategies such as spaced practice, elaboration and dual coding lend themselves very well to our subject and can be linked with retrieval but interleaving is not best suited as part of a well-structured and chronological history curriculum.

Politics

Lucy Ryall

Retrieval practice in politics is not all that different from history. There are key dates, people and examples that have to be recalled and applied to a wide variety of questions. Students also need to know a variety of debates and the different sides of it. The issue with politics, however, is that the facts are endless and every day brings more and more. This can cause a problem. Further to this, politics is all about connections between ideas. Nothing exists in isolation, therefore the retrieval is two-fold. First, students have to recall basic knowledge. Then, they need to apply it in more than one way. One fact or piece of information can be applied in an endless amount of ways. For example, when talking about the powers of the president in the USA, and specifically the impeachment of Trump, this fact comes under multiple headings. You could use it to talk about the lack of power of the president, or the power of congress, or the difference in power between the House of Representatives and the Senate. Students need to be flexible in their application. This skill is marked in Politics and is known as making synoptic links.

Thankfully, there are a variety of strategies that work quite well in politics and can encourage students to think beyond the recall and into the more complex and connected ideas. The best way to start is with simple definition recall – keywords and concepts. I like to use Knowledge Organisers for this as students have a definition readily available and they can learn them in advance. Once these words are known, we tend to move on to making them into a concept map. This involves having around five or six words spread out on a page and students have to make links between them explaining how they interact with each other. This works well in ensuring they understand the keywords or concepts outside of their definition. It also addresses gaps very rapidly. As stated previously, politics requires the use of examples and these need to be as up to date and current as possible, so recall has to go beyond just defining and linking key terms. One way we do this is through presenting an exam question or statement and then providing a list of examples. Students have to select which examples would be used to answer that exam question. This works best when there are only a handful of examples (for example six). You can then expand on their answers, challenge them and use directed questioning to dig into and push students on their reasoning using elaboration.

When doing retrieval in politics, do not assume that because the students are older, they do not need to do the basics. It is important to start at the beginning, with simple retrieval and build it up. If you rush into the more complex retrieval, students will become deflated and this will affect their motivation. Equally, ensure you move on from recall eventually. Just simply defining words or explaining examples means they will lack the ability to apply their knowledge to exam questions. The speed of progression in your retrieval should be based on your students and only when you feel comfortable that they know the basics do you move on.

Lucy Ryall is history teacher and department head for politics at Poole High School. You can follow Lucy on Twitter @LR_History.

Psychology
Louise Rycroft

In psychology, we focus retrieval practice mainly around A01 which is students' knowledge and understanding of key studies, theories and approaches. Within this students are required to know a range of key psychologists and specific facts and figures from the procedures and findings of a variety of research studies. As well as this, when outlining an approach or theory, there is a requirement that students are using key psychological terminology within their answers, all of which provide excellent opportunities to embed retrieval practice into lessons. We are also using retrieval practice as a method for students recalling triggers to support them with their recall of evaluation which is adding depth and detail to their writing.

Within psychology, at DSFC our programme of study has been redesigned to include spaced practice. Psychology has lots of opportunities within the topic areas to create synoptic links such as approaches and psychopathology and research methods and memory, as well as synoptic links between smaller topic areas such as the behaviourist approach to psychology which is also used to explain phobias and also provides the basis for the learning theory of attachment, which allows excellent opportunities for retrieval practice to take place throughout the course. Similarly, with our Year 13 students, we have a focus per half-term on a Year 12 topic so at least one retrieval practice task will be embedded into our lessons based on this.

Retrieval Grids are useful with both with key terminology but can also be question-focused too. Retrieval brain dumps, Kahoot and Quizizz are all widely used within the department. Within psychology we use our knowledge and understanding of how our memory works to support our students with effective revision strategies, finding out what you do not know is just as important as finding out what you *do* know. The key question is then what you are going to do about that missing knowledge and how are you going to embed that within your long-term memory. With a lot of students it is also about building up their confidence of how retrieval practice and key triggers can support your learning and moving students away from 'memorising' information, which is why I try to embed as much practice of retrieval tasks within my lessons so they can see how the strategy works in the real world.

Louise Rycroft is a psychology teacher at Durham Sixth Form Centre (DSFC). I worked with Louise in my previous school. I want to take this opportunity to thank Louise for teaching me so much about memory. It was during the time we worked together that I first became interested in retrieval practice. We presented to colleagues together, Louise explaining key research findings on memory and I shared practical classroom examples. You can follow Louise on Twitter @RycroftLouise.

Design and technology

Nic Edwards

Retrieval in design and technology takes two paths, the retrieval of skills and the retrieval of knowledge. Retrieval practice in a practical context is the very nature of what we do in design and technology, giving students skills and opportunity to develop those skills, each time applying it with more accuracy, precision and expertise. Over the course of a curriculum journey, we naturally impart and model practical skills for our students to develop, and as Rosenshine (2012) states, 'it is simply not enough to present students with new material, because the material will be forgotten unless there is sufficient rehearsal'. Through demonstrating and transferring the skills (material) we give our students opportunities to rehearse and apply their understanding to different contexts. Using a range of materials and specialist techniques will enable students to deepen their ability to work with material or specialist processes with expertise.

However, we can use the retrieval of skill as a hook to develop knowledge and cultural capital linked to that particular skill. For example, in a timber-based project, you can retrieve the practical skills needed furthermore, you can use it as an opportunity to develop knowledge of timbers, specialist techniques and processes, as well as the social and economic impacts of deforestation, and provenance. It is this knowledge that can be retrieved using strategies such as challenge grids, retrieval clocks and multiple-choice questions.

Since the release of the new GCSE design and technology specification in 2017, there has been an increased emphasis on academic rigour, and with that a growing focus on our student's ability to retrieve knowledge from their long-term memory. Retrieval supports the recall of declarative or procedural knowledge. Getting students to retrieve the 'what' before progressing onto the 'how'. Developing a student's ability to retrieve individual strands of knowledge to answer smaller questions enable them to link knowledge and make more progress. For example, retrieving that cotton is a natural fabric, retrieving the life cycle assessment of cotton, retrieving that growing cotton takes a huge amount of water, retrieving that fair trade promotes fair wages and working conditions for their workers enables students to evaluate the social and environmental impact of cotton.

Our department has used many strategies to develop student confidence and ability to retrieve knowledge to improve student outcomes. We use spaced retrieval within our everyday teaching, both in and out of the class. Using curriculum time, we adopt waves of retrieval to support and challenge students' ability to retrieve knowledge. Completing low stakes multiple-choice questions to check student understanding and develop confidence, thinking and linking grids to encourage students to find common links between strands of knowledge, and challenge grids where students are expected to retrieve strands of knowledge to answer exam-style questions. To further support our teaching practices, and embed retrieval within our department, we have adopted Doug Lemov's Teach Like a Champion 2.0 strategies. Using strategies such as no-opt out, show call or pepper to check for understanding after a retrieval task. Using these strategies in conjunction with each other allows our team to identify and address misconceptions within student understanding, closing the gap in their knowledge. Using strategies such as spaced retrieval, waves of retrieval and Doug Lemov's strategies over a series of lessons, term or key stages develops student ability to not only retrieve strands of knowledge but also knit them together to demonstrate a deeper understanding of the subject.

Nic Edwards is a middle leader, curriculum leader of design technology and part of the TeachMeet Design Technology Icons team (@TMDTIcons), where he works with and supports teachers from across the globe. You can follow Nic on Twitter @NED_DT.

Art and design

Fiona Leadbeater

Ten years ago I might have been sceptical of how retrieval practice could be used in art and design. After all, we are a practical subject – hands-on, often highly subjective and very skill-based. Much of the learning which takes place within an art and design department features at the top of Bloom's Taxonomy – high-order thinking skills such as creating, evaluating and analysing artworks and design. In my opinion, that is exactly how it should be. So I'm not about to suggest removing all creativity within the subject and making pupils spend periods writing and memorising facts instead of drawing and designing. Our subject will always be practical. However, back then, my inexperience and lack of understanding might have caused me to write off the need for strong subject knowledge. Perhaps this was because I worried it would distract learners from developing creativity or experiential learning. Having carried out lots of reading on retrieval practice and seen the benefits firsthand for learners in both my art and design and photography classes, I'm now convinced that to achieve success in the high-order skills, learners need the strong foundational knowledge and understanding to support their explorations. I have found retrieval practice an excellent way to improve learners' ability to successfully recall knowledge and in doing so, aid their creativity. So how can retrieval practice be used within a practical subject such as art and design?

I have found that many of the retrieval tasks suggested for non-practical subjects also work well in art and design. I think the key is to think carefully about the knowledge we are hoping to test, and how that knowledge is important in developing practical skills. Determining the 'threshold concepts' within the art and design curriculum is vital in breaking down the knowledge which learners need to be successful in the practical tasks. Colour theory, compositional techniques, properties of art materials, design issues and the visual elements are all important areas of knowledge within the art and design curriculum. Being able to recall this knowledge easily, allows learners to become more confident in developing their own creativity. It frees up their working memory to focus on the complex analysis, evaluative and creating tasks. I have found that this, in turn, leads to more in-depth and sophisticated attempts by pupils to experiment with these concepts and incorporate them into their own work.

The easiest and most effective retrieval practice is often a quick recap quiz which might take the form of questions, writing definitions to keywords or a brain dump about everything pupils can remember about an artist. My pupils love 'Connect 4' which encourages them to answer a series of questions about the visual elements to get four in a row. Retrieval clocks are another good way to improve pupils' vocabulary schema – the context could be colour theory or design issues. It does not matter. The important part is that pupils are thinking hard to retrieve the knowledge from their memory. This is then laying strong foundations for the skills learners need to write about the art world successfully.

Another thing I have learned and am still working to embed fully is the notion that retrieval practice does not just test the knowledge we are covering in our current practical work or project. It is useful to recap learning from last week, last month and last year to allow the learner to build confidence in recalling the knowledge. In art and design, this is fairly straightforward because we often cover similar genres with different year groups but with learners producing alternative outcomes. Therefore, the threshold concepts and core knowledge are often transferable and it is useful to continually revisit this throughout the learner journey. Retrieval practice in art and design could also take the form of a practical 'show me how you know…' task. This may involve the pupil demonstrating a technique or the handling of particular art material. Often our lessons will begin with a starter recap task which allows the learner to retrieve the knowledge they covered last session by actually using the watercolours, or creating a tonal strip to demonstrate their learning of the skill. Retrieval practice does not need to be in written form and could also involve learners testing their memory of a painting by labelling the key compositional techniques or material handling employed by the artist. I would argue that all these retrieval tasks improve art and design learners' ability to access this key knowledge so that they can apply it more confidently, creatively and experimentally.

Fiona Leadbeater is an art and design teacher. You can follow Fiona on Twitter @teachartdesign.

Physical education

Darren Leslie

As a teacher of physical education, I thought long and hard about how I will make use of the many benefits of retrieval practice in my classrooms (including the gym or the track). As our students have so much that they need to remember, such as facts and figures of norms from their various fitness tests and the wide array of factors that impact on their sporting performance, we must utilise the testing effect so that they build up their schemata within their long-term memory. So, I have embedded retrieval practice in several ways in my lessons. I begin every lesson with a quick, low stakes quiz which features knowledge from last lesson, last week, last month and sometimes last year. During classroom-based lessons the students write their responses into their books and then I 'cold call' them to get their responses, this allows the students to self-mark and keeps this part of the lesson as low stakes as possible. In the gymnasium, I ask the questions, offer them some time to think it over and then call on the students to retrieve the information from memory. This is now a key feature of my lessons and the students are very much used to the challenge of retrieving prior knowledge at the beginning of my lessons.

I was conscious that I didn't want retrieval practice to simply be the quiz at the start of the lesson and wanted it to be a feature throughout my lessons. This brought me to using mini-whiteboards (MWB) more regularly. Asking a question and getting students to commit to their answer before showing you is a great tool that is low stakes, but it can have a high impact on learning. It is important here that my questioning is well crafted so that every student has the opportunity to retrieve information from memory and time is given where the students write their responses in silence before my command to show me their boards. This allows me to quickly identify which students are performing well and which students require me to reteach or explain further the material of the lesson. A key strategy that I use with the MWB is 'two things' adapted from *Powerful Teaching* (Agarwal and Bain, 2019), this is where after a sequence of teaching I will ask the students to write down 'two things' that they have just learned. This is a powerful strategy and is slowly becoming a regular occurrence in my classroom.

Darren Leslie is a teacher of PE, he is also the podcast host of Becoming Educated and blogger at becomingeducated.co.uk. You can follow Darren on Twitter @dnleslie.

Music

Felix Hughes

I took over in a new school in January and became responsible for an exam class that lacked confidence with the listening paper. I tried several strategies but nothing would stick, much to mine and their frustration. In reading about the effectiveness of the testing effect – teach, test, test with retrieval practice – I created a series of flashcards on Quizlet. The class completely changed. They really embraced using them each lesson and continued self-testing the flashcards until they had mastered them in the sense that they could confidently recall. The class can be quite competitive so at the end of each lesson we would do a Quizlet Live. Students were retaining the information far better and quicker than they had done previously. There was one point where they simply just wanted to go straight to recall via Quizlet!

It was so successful I created flashcards for every unit of work with Year 10 and asked them to revise at the beginning of each lesson. Comprehension of the key terms improved. However in music, the difficulty is not just in understanding the terms, but being able to identify them in pieces of music. I've started putting multiple-choice exam questions onto Microsoft Forms. I then do a listening test every lesson to check whether students can apply the knowledge, as they are self-marking quizzes. It's easy for me and the students to see where they are doing well and where the gaps are in their knowledge and vocabulary. I had noticed that certain key terms stuck while others were forgotten from one week to the next. I now ask students to use a brain dump (free recall) at the beginning of the lesson to check what has been retained from previous lessons. The classes have all enjoyed using the Cops and Robbers activity from Kate's previous book and we even attempted a remote version using the collaboration space in Class Note on Microsoft Teams.

When we returned after the summer holidays in 2020, most students were getting roughly their target grade in the listening tasks set. After a few weeks though I noticed a couple of students' grades dip quite dramatically. I spoke to one student to try to work out why. I set her the task of revising the material she had got wrong. When I came back there were highlighted and underlined sections all over the place! In class, I have asked students to put key terms in a table, with a diagram, definition and a box for any memory hooks. I asked her to go back and self-quiz, covering one column and trying to recall the others. Her next test was back to her target grade. My students and I have realised the benefits of retrieval practice in this subject – to assume this technique does not lend itself well to music is an incorrect assumption many students can make.

Felix Hughes is a music teacher and Director of Performance Faculty at Sir John Talbot's School in Whitchurch, Shropshire. I had the privilege of working with Felix in Wales. He is an enthusiastic teacher and leader who leads by example and never stops learning and reflecting. You can follow Felix on Twitter @felixhughes6.

Business

Jade Lewis-Jones

For students selecting Business at GCSE or A Level, it is often a brand new subject. There is a large amount of terminology for students to learn, command words to process and different exam skills to understand. Retrieval practice is essential in this subject. Picture Prompts are a fabulous way of supporting students when building an understanding of a particular topic, the following graphic is an example of this for 'Location Factors'. This is great for differentiating too, some students could have less pictures, others could have the first letter of the word added. This is a way of triggering students' memories and boosting their confidence. It is also helpful for me as a teacher to highlight particular aspects where students have gaps in their knowledge and which aspects need revisiting.

Retrieval practice – picture prompt

Next to each image explain how they could impact the business's choice of where it could locate.

I highly rate using brain dumps. I have used these for all year groups but I find they are particularly useful with Year 11 and Year 13 students when asking them to recap over content covered in the first year of the course. What I love about brain dumps is that students are not rushed – they have time to write down everything they know on the unit, chapter or topic that we are focusing on. This is also good to assess what students already know on a topic before teaching them, a great way of assessing progress! As Kate champions, these are 'low effort, high impact' tasks for students to complete. I have recently completed this with a Year 11 class on completion of the marketing unit - where the hope is that they not only write definitions or key terms but also draw illustrations to show the different distribution channels, draw the product life cycle and label the different stages. The useful part of this retrieval method is that it allows the more able students to explore the advantages and disadvantages of different pricing strategies, for example, or to delve a little deeper into their analysis and evaluation abilities with elaboration.

At A Level, time can be tight to ensure that students understand the command words, the exam structure and the content being covered, teachers regularly feel under pressure to get the theory taught. The focus of the Business A Level has a lot of emphasis on longer essays, however, it's good to break up lessons, and ensure student engagement with interactive quizzes such as Kahoot or Quizizz. Students really enjoy these as they can use their own devices and it allows them to test their knowledge of definitions and such, creating a really fun atmosphere amongst the students. It serves as a low stakes form of revision to prepare them for the final high stakes exam.

Jade Lewis-Jones is assistant academic headteacher and teacher of business at an international school in Spain. Jade and I worked together in Wales before we both decided to teach internationally. Jade has always been a great source of professional inspiration and support for me. You can follow Jade on Twitter @educationjade.

Economics

Sarah Jones

Students often take up economics as an option relatively late in their school career. As such, they have to get used to being complete novices again and this can affect the confidence of some who are used to being relative experts in other subjects. I use retrieval practice from very early in any economics course to build confidence and help to rapidly bring up student skills and knowledge from a novice position. Microeconomics: students of microeconomics need to master a vast amount of precise definitions and diagrams to succeed. Their task is somewhat comparable to needing to master phonics to ultimately be able to read *War and Peace* – they have to learn the specific language and many conventions of the subject.

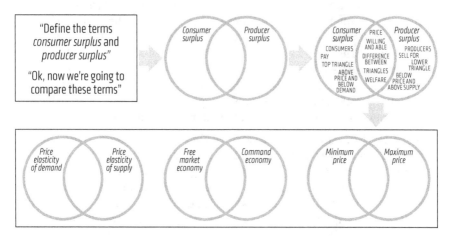

For complex diagrams, particularly those relating to demand, supply and theory of the firm, I typically teach only a few single curves or simple diagrams at time. I then frequently ask novice students to sketch them from memory on mini-whiteboards at the start of lessons. I ensure they understand and can recall them securely before moving on to add further curves and complexity. After teaching complete, complex diagrams, I chop up diagram learning sheets into call cards and regularly randomly select one or two from a box on my desk for mini-whiteboard retrieval. I enjoy increasing the level of challenge further by asking more experienced students to process and manipulate diagrams (examining different areas on complex static diagrams or moving curves around) to develop their ability to use diagrams as an expert to analyse real-world issues.

Macroeconomics: understanding macroeconomics requires students to remember many processes such as how changes in interest rates work their way through to affect indicators such as inflation, growth or employment. I often use flow charts to teach these processes, so retrieval will typically involve me displaying flow charts I have previously taught with blank boxes in and then asking students to try to complete the chains in the chart from memory. Again, this can build from a very simple novice 'which step is missing?' type questions, right up to requiring students to recall full paragraphs of traditional theoretical analysis or evaluation with no visual clues. Using visuals in teaching and retrieval of macroeconomic concepts has been crucial in being able to convey my thinking to students to build their expertise and skills in thinking independently as economists themselves.

Sarah Jones is a subject leader for business, economics and finance. She is also coordinator of independent learning and a specialist leader of education at Redborne Upper School and Community College. You can follow Sarah on Twitter @JonesLearnUK and visit her blog joneslearnUK.blogspot.com.

Computer science

Gemma Moine

In recent years, educational research has narrowed its lens on the findings of cognitive psychology and retrieval practice. Understanding research and translating this into how this could look like in a computer science classroom proved tricky initially. On reflection, it was simplifying the activities into quick, straightforward unambiguous tasks that served as the starting point for success in delivery. Many of the brilliant shared ideas for retrieval practice activities are amazing but not necessarily fit for purpose for every subject. The computer science department experimented and put together a simple toolbox of activities that worked for the subject and were easy to embed into the classroom. I have shared below some of my favourites.

Mystery object: Place a device/computer part on the desk before students enter the room, you can make several stations around the room either with the same or different mystery object. Split students into small groups and allocate a workstation. Either on a large piece of paper or if desks are wipeable use whiteboard pens to recall as much as they can about that object/topic. This task takes no time to set up and the mystery object could include:

- a stick of RAM (links to discussions about primary storage, function of RAM).

- an old network switch (links to discussion on networking, packet switching, MAC addresses, topology).

- different types of wires (links to discussions on parallel and serial transmission, simplex/full duplex, advantages/disadvantages of different types).

- a CPU chip (linking to computer architecture, buses, registers and FDE cycle).

- binary dice (links to binary, denary, hexadecimals, data transmission, check sum, check digit, 2s complement, floating point, the list could go on...).

Students write down what they can recall or they could create a drawing including the object, for example, the switch in the centre of a star topology diagram. Students have five minutes max to complete the task and the teacher visits each group and, through discussion, the group can identify if there are any areas of revision needed. You can also include some non-technical mystery objects for fun. I have used an old 'bunch of balloons' plastic attachment and students linked it to parallel transmission with the multiple lines of data travelling through the small pipes instead of water.

Talk to the duck! Many computer science classrooms have adopted and encouraged students to independently debug code by talking through their code with the aid of the faithful rubber duck! Talking through algorithms out loud, line by line, helps students identify logical errors in their programs. Make the duck part of an easy retrieval task by asking students to talk through what they learnt last lesson, last week or last term to the duck. By recalling past learning frequently in this way we realised that students were able to recall knowledge quickly and without prompters. Pro-tip: use a screwdriver to remove the squeak!

Gemma Moine is a computer science teacher and my colleague at The British School Al Khubairat in Abu Dhabi. Gemma authored *Knowledge Quiz: Computer Science*, which is part of a series of knowledge quizzes published for schools.

Sociology

Carly Benge

Sociology is not only packed full of factual content to remember but requires students to demonstrate skills (assessment objectives) such as knowledge and understanding, application, analysis and evaluation. Students are also expected to draw upon their knowledge from more than one unit of study and demonstrate synoptic links between them when answering particular exam questions. Daily retrieval practice has been a game-changer for me and my students in developing confidence and subject knowledge.

A great activity for sociology is the thinking and linking grid. This is fantastic for making my students find a wider range of connections between concepts. Examples of topics I have created thinking and linking grids on are science and ideology, 'is religion a conservative force or a force for change' debate and class differences in educational achievement (internal and external factors). I have recently been adapting my questioning technique when reviewing this particular activity to encourage students to use their 'chain of reasoning skills' instead of just telling me the link and why. I encourage them through questioning to break down their answer into more detailed chunks to demonstrate their ability to analyse. I then model these answers on the board to highlight the difference between a lower band piece of writing and a top band piece of writing. Another activity can be seen with the following keyword spotlight grid.

Name:

Keyword spotlight grid: religion as a conservative force (Marxism)

Keyword	Definition	Use the term correctly in a sentence	Create a question where the keyword is the answer	Draw a picture to show the keyword	Other keywords linked to the keyword
Conserve					
Ideology					
Status quo					
False class consciousness					
Justify					

I ensure that I regularly refer back to previous knowledge through spaced practice. Kate's Retrieval Practice Challenge Grid has been brilliant for this and I aim to use it at least twice per half-term with all of my classes. Shoutout to @HecticTeacher for her weekly rolling retrieval quizzes, which I use with my Year 13s to re-cap Year 12 content. The Hectic Teacher repeats half of the questions in the quiz the following week to ensure that learning of the content has happened. She also gets students to plot their own graph of progress on these quizzes so they can take ownership of their learning.

Finally, focusing retrieval on keywords and dual coding is valuable for sociology and something that I like to do regularly in my classes. I find that retrieval naturally happens at the beginning of my lessons as a 'starter' activity, however, now I am more confident with it, I am looking to vary when this happens in future lessons to ensure maximum impact on the students.

Carly Benge is a social sciences teacher for both AQA A Level and GCSE. You can follow Carly on Twitter @CarlyMBenge.

Drama

Jemma Stilwell

I am grateful to be working at such a wonderful school which embeds educational research and practice. It was here that I discovered the term retrieval practice and it made me start to develop a new way of thinking about how my students retain and recall information. This has become a massive focus in drama due to the new content-heavy specifications and we are now asking students to not only be fantastic actors but to have a theoretical understanding of theatre design and pedagogical practices of practitioners.

At Key Stage 3 it is quite normal to have one drama lesson a week. The students usually have not studied the key skills in primary school and it is essentially starting from scratch with keywords, meanings and theatre history. There is so much content to be covered in such a short space of time so I use the retrieval grids. I found it the best way to embed drama vocabulary and skills in a combined format and getting students to think beyond the lesson they were being taught. An example follows:

What is the definition of a 'still image' in drama?	What is the purpose of using cross cutting in a devised piece of theatre?	What is the 'physical theatre' in its broadest term? Can you give an example of when you have used it?	What is a mime?
What is direct address?	What is 'thought tracking' in drama?	What do we mean by style in drama?	What genre was the last text/theme/issue we studied?
What is a monologue?	What does the word 'gait' mean?	What is hot seating and why is it a useful tool?	What are the different forms of drama?
1 point	2 points	3 points	4 points

What I love about the retrieval grids is how adaptable they are once you have made them. You can use them at any point in a lesson and I have found it useful to get the students to extend their answers and form a discussion as a class. A strategy that links the grid to a practical task is to dedicate one set of boxes to different techniques. Students can then get up and show me practically what each one looks like. For instance, they may know what a mime is, but do they know how to make a successful one? I would ask the students to then get up practically and show me what an effective one looks like and as an incentive I always give them more points. This then builds a discussion on what an effective 'still image' or 'mime' is and allows the students to reflect on great practice. Another technique I used early on in my career was something called a 'word race'. During drama I usually get the students into teams of around four or five and then into a line ready for a race. I place a piece of paper at the end with one marker pen. I ask students to write down as much as they can about the topic we have been studying. This can include drama techniques, context, characters, subtext, but they must not repeat anything else anyone has written. I also place a time limit on the activity to increase quick-thinking skills. You can also see them preparing their answers in the line, which I always enjoy watching. This activity allows you to deal with any misconceptions and ask questions about some of the answers on the page.

As a middle leader, I have always found that all teachers struggle with fitting new ways of working into their already well-rehearsed way of teaching with GCSE. After reading so much about the impact retrieval can have on students, I really wanted it to work in my department. I did not want the idea of it to become something that made my team feel as though the tasks were not working or that they did not have time to cover content, so I had to begin thinking about how I plan for retrieval practice, especially for the students taking exams. When it comes to planning for retrieval Shaun Allison and Andy Tharby (2015) suggested the two following questions:

1. Which ideas and concepts are absolutely crucial to the overall mastery of the topic?

2. How many opportunities to return to these ideas in different contexts can you include in the plan?

Thinking about GCSE drama and the play *Blood Brothers*, my mind was immediately drawn to the context and political themes within the play. This is what drives the characters and ultimately leads to their demise. I then had to stop myself and think about the overall course. What are the key concepts in every component? How can I link them together so that the retrieval activity gets students to focus on the key skills of evaluating and analysing drama? I want the students to recognise the links in every aspect of their course, not just the play they are currently studying. This then led me to think about interleaving and spaced practice. This train of thought made me completely change my approach to firstly the timetabling of the course and secondly the real key in succeeding in the drama exam. We have two members of full-time staff and instead of each person taking a GCSE class, we decided to teach them both. What this has allowed us to do is teach two components of the exam simultaneously and set out the key concepts into sections:

Week	Teacher 1 – *Blood Brothers*	Teacher 2 – Live theatre
1-3	Social, cultural and political context	Social, cultural and political context
4-7	Characters thoughts feelings and emotions Drama vocal and physical skills	Characters thoughts feelings and emotions Drama vocal and physical skills
8-14	Set, props, lighting, sound, costume, hair and makeup	Set, props, lighting, sound, costume, hair and makeup

As you can see, we are both teaching the same skills, but using a different text or play. By doing this the students can make connections and helped us to implement retrieval for the overall course. I liked doing a retrieval activity once every two weeks as I felt it was enough time to reflect and act upon what they may have forgotten, but also a chance to learn new content. All of the ideas have come from Kate's first book and are easily adaptable for any subject.

Week	Retrieval practice task
3	Retrieval grid
5	Retrieval practice placemat
7	List it! (Referring to all the physical and vocal skills)
9	Multiple choice test
11	Thinking and linking grid
13	Retrieval grid

The following is an example of my thinking and linking grid, where students have to use dice and then make links between the different factors selected. As a drama teacher, it was always interesting to see how the students make connections between different characters from two different plays. What they usually ended up doing was discussing the contrast between the way the character would use physical and vocal skills, which is exactly what I wanted them to do! The following grid is based upon *Blood Brothers* and *Things I Know To Be True*.

	1	2	3	4	5	6
1	Social class	Trust	Pip	Direct address	Linda	Audience
2	Mental health	Politics	Aims	Costume	Eddie	Guilt
3	Family	Proxemics	Education	Subtext	Tension	Fran
4	Style	Props	Physical Theatre	Crime	Lighting	Empathy
5	Context	Mickey	Sound	Contrast	Atmosphere	Destiny
6	Set	Mark	Cyclical structure	Divide	Hair and makeup	Nature vs nurture

Jemma Stilwell is Director of Drama at Dubai College in the United Arab Emirates. You can follow Jemma on Twitter @TalksDrama.

Modern Foreign Languages (MFL)

Barry Smith

I don't know what 'retrieval practice' even means, but I think I know what effective and ineffective teaching looks like. Ineffective teaching is a teacher 'covering' a topic. The teacher talks, some kids listen, some kids even understand, momentarily, then the teacher moves on to the next topic. The teaching lacked precision; high-frequency errors were not tackled head-on; the roots of misconceptions were not really addressed; explanations were meandering; key points were poorly made and, understandably, will not be retained by kids. Next lesson, scant reference will be made to what was taught last lesson, last term or last year. Memories, not secure in the first place, quickly fade. This cycle repeats. Topic 'covered'. Next topic 'covered'. Little reference made to links between topics. Kids retain little. Topic will be 'covered' again in a few months, according to the scheme of work (SOW). You must, above all else, stick to the SOW. That must never be questioned. And, in a few months, when we revisit the topic, it feels like starting all over again from zero. Kids feel thick. Teachers are left frustrated. In French, the only subject I feel I can speak on with any semblance of authority, what is touted as good practice is – I would contend, too often – very bad practice indeed.

Neatly compartmentalised topics mean vocabulary is presented then put aside, rather than recycled and truly remembered. Inevitably, even if this compartmentalised language becomes part of pupils' passive vocabulary, it too rarely transfers to their active vocabulary. So, I advocate very loose adherence to topics and lots of revisiting and recycling of language across topics so kids don't 'nearly' learn, they 'really' learn, the language they have been exposed to. I talk about 80/20. Very roughly, when presenting new language, only around 20% of the language is truly new. The rest is recycled language we have already encountered. That is, in part, why I teach blocks of text rather than disparate words. And what does 'new' even mean? There are only 26 letters in the alphabet. The same letter combinations are used over and over. They're easily recognisable. French is full of patterns and is very logical if you know where to look. So, effective teachers teach kids patterns, how highly predictable the language is. In that way, kids encounter 'new' language but understand, nothing is really 'new'. It's just the same old patterns repeating.

As for grammar, teachers just teach too much of it, very often. The grammar is 'covered' but it isn't practised enough so it never thoroughly embeds. Of course, teaching phonics in French, light touch, nothing too complex, could preempt so many of the issues kids have learning French grammar. And then there's the focus on games and variety. I think the concept is, motivate kids through 'fun' activities. I'm going to call that *'la charrue avant les boeufs'*. Teach kids so they feel they are making rapid progress, use the most time effective strategies at your disposal, only use activities that offer an excellent learning return on time invested. Do not worry about 'fun', worry about kids feeling accomplished.

Motivation comes from feeling successful. Run towards the high-frequency errors. Preempt these errors. Gain lesson time. Use that time to ensure that language taught last week, month, term, year, is recycled and retained forever in both kids' passive and active personal lexicon.

Barry Smith is former Deputy Headteacher at Michaela Community School and is Regional Director, Community Schools Trust. I have watched Barry teach and he is an incredible teacher. I have had many conversations with him about teaching and learning, he has helped me a lot and at times challenged my ideas and approaches. You can follow Barry on Twitter @BarryNSmith79.

A huge thank you to the wonderful teachers and contributors for sharing their advice and reflections about retrieval practice in this chapter.

On the topic of subject specialism, do you use retrieval practice as a strategy to support and develop your subject knowledge? There have been occasions in my career where I have had to teach content (or even whole subjects!) where my background prior knowledge was very basic. I would resort to re-reading and making endless notes but now I practice what I preach and I do use retrieval practice to develop and deepen my subject knowledge. If I am reading a chapter of a book, I will create questions based on the text and record the answers on a separate sheet of paper. I will allow some time to pass and then self-test. Despite creating the questions myself there are always questions

I cannot recall the answers to. This is not a problem, this is useful as (just like I would tell my students) I know where the gaps are in my knowledge and I will act on that. Perhaps this is common or perhaps some teachers are encouraging their students to use effective study strategies but they continue to highlight, underline and re-read.

I hope this book has given you a lot of food for thought as well as some practical advice and strategies to directly implement in your classroom. I will keep learning, reflecting and sharing when it comes to retrieval practice in the classroom. We are certainly not there yet but together, academics, teachers and leaders, we are all heading in a very positive direction.

References

Agarwal, P. K. and Bain, P. M. (2019) *Powerful Teaching: Unleash the Science of Learning.* San Francisco: Jossey-Bass.

Chi, M. T. H., Feltovich, P. J. and Glaser, R. (1981) 'Categorization and Representation of Physics Problems by Experts and Novices', *Cognitive Science* 5 (2) pp. 121-152.

McGrane, C. and McCourt, M. (2020) *Mathematical Tasks: The Bridge Between Teaching and Learning.* Woodbridge: John Catt Educational.

Rohrer, D., Dedrick, R. F. and Agarwal, P. K. (2007) *Interleaved Mathematics Practice: Giving Students a Chance to Learn What They Need to Know.* Retrieved from: www.bit.ly/3aW6HPD

Rosenshine, B. (2012) 'Principles of Instruction', American Educator 36 (1) pp. 12-19.

Siegler, R. S. (2003) 'Implications of cognitive science research for mathematics education'. In J. Kilpatrick, W. G. Martin and D. E. Schifter. (Eds.), *A research companion to principles and standards for school mathematics* (pp. 119-233). Reston, VA: National Council of Teachers of Mathmatics.

Tharby, A. and Allison, S. (2015) *Making Every Lesson Count: Six Principles to Support Great Teaching and Learning.* Carmarthen: Crown House Publishing

Online resources

Here you can access all my blog posts about retrieval practice and teaching and learning.
lovetoteach87.com

This is my TES resources homepage where you can download my 'Effective Strategies' study guide as well as templates to all my retrieval practice resources for free.
tes.com/member/K8SUE

This is the link to the free 'A Brief Introduction to Retrieval Practice' course I designed with Seneca Learn and you will receive a certificate on completion.
bit.ly/3sfh7jH

This is Adam Boxer's website where you can read his blog and find out more about his Retrieval Roulette concept.
achemicalorthodoxy.wordpress.com

CPSIA information can be obtained
at www.ICGtesting.com
Printed in the USA
JSHW041701070221
11557JS00003B/4